Ian Dawson was born and raised in Hathersage in the heart of the Peak District. Since an early age he has been keen on sport, the outdoor life and local geography, spending nearly three years guiding people around the Castleton caves. An enthusiastic traveller, he has spent time in Australia and Indonesia. Following a degree in Public Administration his working life has been spent in sales and marketing. This is his first book.

Following page
Ashover church (see No 120)

EXPLORING
around
SOUTH YORKSHIRE

Ian Dawson

THE DOVECOTE PRESS

To Mickey

First published in 1994 by The Dovecote Press Ltd
Stanbridge, Wimborne, Dorset BH21 4JD

ISBN 1 874336 24 5

© Ian Dawson 1994

Phototypeset in Times by The Typesetting Bureau
Wimborne, Dorset
Printed and bound by Biddles Ltd
Guildford and Kings Lynn

CONTENTS

INTRODUCTION

The area around Sheffield, from Wakefield in the north to Matlock in the south, from Chapel en le Frith in the west to Retford in the east, is rich in culture, geography, art and entertainment. *Exploring Around South Yorkshire* is my selection of just under two hundred ways to experience the region at its best. If you enjoy using it as much as I enjoyed writing it then all the hard work will have been worthwhile. I have included at the end of each entry other local sites of interest as suggestions to continue your explorations – you may find others. I hope you enjoy them too.

Many people have helped me in the compilation of this book and I would like to thank the following. Firstly, Duncan Smith for his help and encouragement throughout the planning and writing of this book, his guidance and publishing expertise has been invaluable. To David Burnett of the Dovecote Press for giving me the chance to publish my work. Also, Simon Laffoley for the photographs and his endless enthusiasm, to Trevor Croucher for the cover photographs, and Bob Dawson for his literary guidance. Finally, I should like to thank Rachel for her help, understanding and patience, and my family and friends for their support. For permission to take photographs: English Heritage (Conisbrough Castle, Roche Abbey, Monk Bretton Priory and Peveril Castle), The Ivanhoe Trust (Conisbrough Castle), The National Trust (Winster Market House), and The Yorkshire Sculpture Park and Igor Mitoraj (Thsuki-No-Hikari).

Ian Dawson

Key to Symbols

Admission Prices: (per person)
A – below £3.00
B – £3.00 to £6.00
C – Above £6.00.

Facilities

   Disabled Facilities (may vary in each case, please telephone to confirm.)

wc Toilets.

Refreshments available.

℗ Parking available.

s Shop available.

Please note that whilst every attempt has been made to confirm that the information given is correct, the publishers do not accept any responsibility for alterations or inaccuracies.

Where no facilities, opening times or admission prices are listed it is assumed that they are not applicable.

Whilst a map reference and brief directions are given to each entry it is recommended that this guide book is used in conjunction with a good, up to date road atlas and the following Ordnance Survey Landranger maps; 110, 111, 119, 120.

Map

The reference in brackets given after each entry refers to the map on pages 8 and 9.

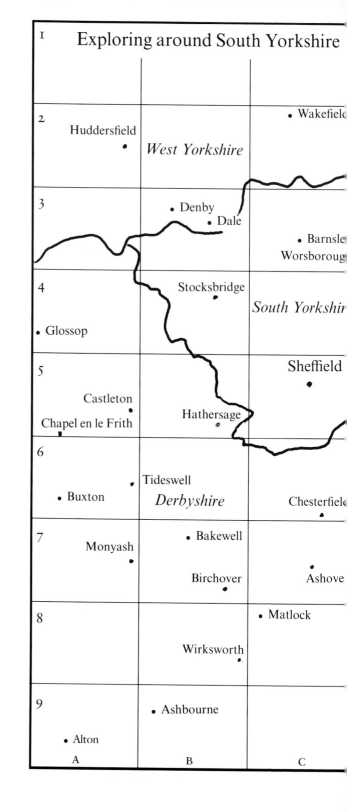

Exploring around South Yorkshire

1

2
Huddersfield
West Yorkshire
• Wakefield

3
• Denby
• Dale
• Barnsley
Worsborough

4
Stocksbridge
South Yorkshire
• Glossop

5
Castleton
Chapel en le Frith
Hathersage
Sheffield

6
Tideswell
• Buxton
Derbyshire
Chesterfield

7
Monyash
• Bakewell
Birchover
Ashover

8
• Matlock
Wirksworth

9
• Ashbourne
• Alton

A   B   C

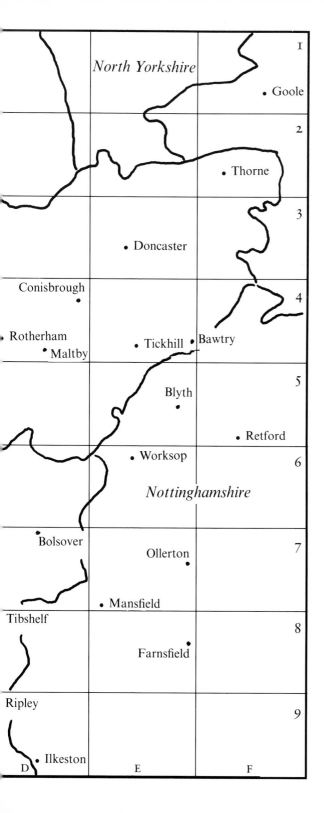

HISTORIC BUILDINGS
INDUSTRIAL HERITAGE
MUSEUMS AND GALLERIES

1. Abbeydale Industrial Hamlet (C5)

A restored scythe works, the site and many of its buildings date back to the mid-18th century. Powered by four waterwheels driven by the River Sheaf, the Hamlet is now a museum where visitors are able to step back in time and see machines and workshops restored to their original condition, including a water driven tilt forge and a Huntsman crucible furnace. An old warehouse block contains a display illustrating the industrial development of Sheffield.

Price: A. (Concessions; OAP, children, families).
Facilities: ℗ ⌂ wc s ♿
Open: All year except over Christmas period, Tuesday to Saturday 10am-5pm, Sunday 11am-5pm.
Situated: Four miles south-west of central Sheffield.
Nearby: 4, 59, 99, 161.   ☎ (0742) 367731

2. Bakewell Church (B7)

Situated in a small market town, the home of the Bakewell pudding, the parish church of All Saints stands halfway up the hill on the west side of town. Although the steeple was rebuilt in the mid-19th century, much of the building dates back to the Norman era (12th century). However, a Saxon cross in the graveyard suggests that there was a church here as early as the 8th century. In the Vernon chapel can be seen monuments to the Vernon and Manners families. Sir George Vernon (died 1567) was known as "King of the Peak" because of his extravagant lifestyle and the lavish hospitality he provided at nearby Haddon Hall.

Open: Daily, Summer 9am-5pm, Winter 9am-4pm.
Situated: Bakewell, on A6 between Matlock and Buxton.
Nearby: 3, 25, 136, 143.

3. Bakewell Old House Museum (B7)

A museum of local antiquities situated in the oldest house in town. Originally a parsonage (dated 1543), the Tudor building was converted into tenements at the end of the 18th century, before finally being restored to its original wattle and daub interior by the Bakewell Historical Society in 1959. It houses a collection of "folk" exhibits, including a restored Victorian kitchen, costume displays, old children's toys, craftmen's tools and laces.

Price: A. (Concessions; children).
Open: April to October, daily 2pm-5pm.
Situated: Cunningham Place, Bakewell, off the A6 between Matlock and Buxton.
Nearby: 2, 25, 136, 143.   ☎ (0629) 813647

4. Beauchief Abbey (C5)

Now a ruin with just the west tower remaining, the Abbey originally dates back to 1175 when it was built by an offshoot of the Augustinian order of monks. Standing in delightful gardens, the Abbey has been well preserved since the 17th century.

Price: Free.
Situated: Off the A621 south-west of central Sheffield.
Nearby: 1, 59, 99, 161.

Beauchief Abbey.

Boston Castle.

5. Boston Castle (D4)

A square, two-storied building standing on one of Rotherham's highest points, Boston Castle was built as a shooting lodge by the Earl of Effingham to mark his opposition to British attempts to crush the American Revolution in 1775. Named after the Boston Tea Party, it is said that the Earl forbade tea being drunk inside its walls. Not open to the public, but the surrounding gardens are worth exploring.

> **Situated:** Rotherham town centre overlooking the A630. Access is via Boston Castle Grove off Moorgate road.
> **Nearby:** 16, 76, 131, 137.

6. Bishops' House Museum (C5)

Originating in the 15th century, with extensions in both the 16th and 17th centuries, this timber-framed Tudor yeoman's house stands as the finest example of its kind in Sheffield. Much of the house has been restored to its original state. Furnished rooms with original and period furniture allow the visitor a glimpse back into Sheffield life during Tudor and Stuart times.

> **Price:** A.
> **Facilities:** wc &
> **Open:** All year, Wednesday to Saturday 10am-4.30pm, Sunday 11am-4.30pm.
> **Situated:** Two miles south of central Sheffield on A621.
> **Nearby:** 4, 43, 89, 104. ☎ (0742) 557701

Bishops' House Museum.

7. Boiler House Gallery (D4)

Uniquely sited in the old school boiler house, the gallery was initiated by the school art teacher to display three and two dimensional contemporary art, by both local and national artists.

Price: Free.
Open: During school term time, Monday to Friday 10am-2pm.
Situated: Maltby Comprehensive School, on A631 east of Rotherham.
Nearby: 51, 131, 146, 147.　　　　　☏ (0709) 812864

8. Bolsover Castle (D7)

The first castle on this site was built by William the Conqueror for his son, however, little of this Norman building remains. What we see today was built in the 17th century by Sir Charles Cavendish in a medieval fortified style, more for romantic attraction than for practical or defensive reasons, continued in the same vein by his son William Cavendish, the first Duke of Newcastle. The site includes a 17th century riding school,

Bolsover Castle.

ruins from the original castle, and inside the building, delightful wall paintings, Jacobean panelling and intricately carved marble fireplaces. Its impressive positioning and panoramic views over the Vale of Scarsdale make it the ideal setting for the operas which are held there periodically. An English Heritage property.

Price: B. (Concessions; OAP, children, party rates, English Heritage members free).

Facilities: ⒮ ♿ (limited), ⓟ 🅆🅒

Open: 1 April to 30 September, daily 10am-6pm, 1 October to 31 March, Tuesday to Sunday 10am-4pm.

Situated: Bolsover, east of Chesterfield.

Nearby: 15, 63, 105, 122. ☎ (0246) 823349

9. Buxton Museum and Art Gallery (A6)

The highlight of the museum is the "Wonders of the Peak" gallery (for which it won Museum of the Year in 1990) featuring local geology and archaeology from pre-history to the present day complete with sounds and smells! Upstairs is the art gallery, where, in addition to prints, pottery and glass, are found collections of ornaments made from local stone (Blue John and Ashford Marble).

Price: A. (Concessions; UB40, OAP, under 5 free, families).

Facilities: 🅆🅒 ♿ ⓟ (limited)

Open: All year except Bank Holidays, Tuesday to Friday 9.30am-5.30pm, Saturday 9.30am-5pm.

Situated: Terrace Road, Buxton.

Nearby: 10, 81, 123, 186. ☎ (0298) 24658

Buxton Opera House.

10. Buxton Opera House (A6)

The last building in the Buxton gardens complex to be completed. It was built in 1905 to the design of the theatre architect Frank Mateham, subsequently fell into disuse and, prior to its restoration in 1979 to the original classical and art nouveau state, was used as a cinema. It is now the focal point for the Buxton International Arts Festival and regularly holds musical and performing arts concerts. Tours available with advance booking.

Price: On application, according to the event.
Facilities: wc ℗
Situated: Buxton town centre.
Nearby: 9, 81, 123, 186.   ☎ (0298) 721290

11. Castleton Church (A5)

Dating back to the Norman era, the Parish Church of St Edmund was originally built by the Peverel family at about the time they built the local castle. However, much of the present building dates from restoration work carried out in 1837. During the spring a garland of flowers is hoisted up the spire as the final act of Garland Day. The origin of this ceremony may well be a pre-Christian celebration heralding the end of winter, but in the 17th century the festival was adapted to celebrate the end of Oliver Cromwell's Commonwealth and the return of Charles II.

Open: 9am to dusk Monday to Saturday, Sunday from 8am.
Situated: Castleton, west of Sheffield on A625.
Nearby: 12, 44, 154, 182.

12. Castleton Village Museum (A5)

Illustrates local village life through the ages, including displays on Peveril Castle, lead mining and Garland day.

Price: A. (Concessions; children, OAP).
Facilities: Ⓟ
Open: Sundays and some weekdays, May to October. Other times by appointment.
Situated: Castleton Methodist church rooms, west of Sheffield on A625.
Nearby: 11, 44, 154, 174.   ☎ (0433) 620518

13. Catcliffe Glass Cone (C5)

The oldest surviving kiln of its type in Western Europe and one of only four in the United Kingdom. Built in 1740 for William Fenney, who ran the glass works at Bolsterstone, its original usage ceased in the late 19th century. Since then it has been used to house prisoners of war during the First World War and as a children's canteen during the industrial disputes of 1926.

Situated: Catcliffe, on the side of the A630 to the north-east of Sheffield.
Nearby: 69, 129, 177, 198.

*Catcliffe
Glass Cone.*

16

Chatsworth House.

14. Chatsworth House (B7)

The home of the Duke and Duchess of Devonshire, the first house was built on this site in the mid-16th century, although nothing of the original buildings remains other than the Hunting Tower in the woods overlooking the house, and Queen Mary's Bower in the grounds by the River Derwent. The present "Palace of the Peak" was begun in the late 17th century by the first Duke of Devonshire and was continued through the years by further generations of Devonshires, notably the sixth Duke who made extensive additions in the 1820s. The interior of the house is rich and palatial – huge rooms with painted ceilings, classical statues, rare furniture and fine paintings. The gardens are equally impressive. Although their present layout owes much to Capability Brown, they owe more to the skill of the sixth Duke's gardener, Joseph Paxton. It was he who was responsible for the spectacular gravity-fed Emperor Fountain and many more of the garden's beautiful features. Next to the house can be found the estate farm, also open to visitors. (see 84)

Price: B. (Concessions; OAP, students, children, families, group bookings).
Facilities: ℗ [wc] [s] ⅙ (garden only)
Open: 21 March to 31 October, 11am-4.30pm.
Situated: North of Matlock on the B6012.
Nearby: 84, 126, 138, 167.　　　　　☏ (0246) 582204

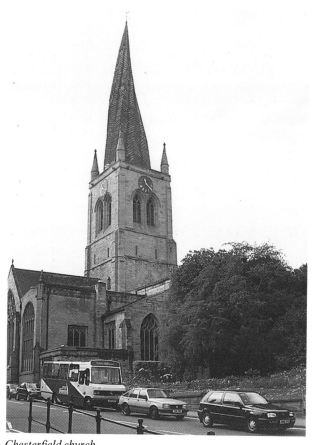

Chesterfield church.

15. Chesterfield Church (C6)

St Mary and All Saints Church owes much of its fame to the curious, crooked spire. Although there are many stories to explain its twisted look, the Black Death is probably most to blame. It was rife throughout the land whilst the church was being built in the 14th century and as a result many local craftsmen died. Those who survived continued the work, but in their naivety used green timbers which over the years have warped. Inside can be seen some fine church brasses, a beautiful 18th century candelabra, and an elegant Renaissance screen.

Open: All year
Situated: Chesterfield town centre.
Nearby: 46, 50, 124, 160.

16. Clifton Park Museum (D4)

Originally an ironfounder's mansion, dating back to 1783. It opened as a museum in 1893 and now houses a collection of local and national artefacts including Roman antiquities from a fort at nearby Templeborough, a large quantity of the local Rockingham ware pottery and period furnished rooms.

Facilities: Ⓟ |wc| ♿

Open: All year, Monday to Thursday and Saturday 10am-5pm, Sunday 2.30pm-5pm.

Situated: Clifton Park, Rotherham, south-east of central Rotherham.

Nearby: 5, 76, 131, 137.   ☏ (0709) 371602

17. Conisbrough Castle (D4)

Built in the 12th century on the site of an existing Saxon settlement, it is one of the finest examples of Norman defensive architecture in the country and has the oldest surviving circular keep in England. Enlarged throughout the 13th and 14th centuries it fell into disuse at the end of Henry VIII's reign. Much of the chapel and other integral parts of the castle remain, however, to give a good impression of life in the Middle Ages. An English Heritage property.

Price: A. (Concessions; OAP, UB40, children, groups, English Heritage members free).

Facilities: |s| |wc| Ⓟ ♿ (limited)

Open: 1 April to 30 September 10am-6pm, 1 October to 31 March 10am-4pm.

Situated: On A630, south-west of Doncaster.

Nearby: 7, 30, 35, 114.   ☏ (0709) 863329

18. Cooper Art Gallery (C3)

Houses a constantly changing programme of exhibitions of fine contemporary art and craft, and the permanent Cooper art collection of 17th, 18th and 19th century European paintings.

Price: Free.

Facilities: ♿ |wc|

Open: Wednesday to Saturday 10am-5.30pm, Tuesday 1pm-5.30pm.

Situated: Church Street, central Barnsley.

Nearby: 36, 74, 98, 119.   ☏ (0226) 242905

19. Cromford Mills (C8)

The world's first successful water-powered cotton mill, built by Sir Richard Arkwright in 1771, and responsible for turning Cromford into one of England's first industrial villages. Cotton milling stopped in Cromford in 1846, since when the mill has had various uses. Since 1979 a restoration programme has been carried out on many of the buildings, which now house exhibitions on Cromford and Arkwright. Nearby can be found Willersley Castle, the home of Sir Richard Arkwright, and the Cromford bridge, a stone in which commemorates a feat of 1697 when a man on horseback jumped unharmed into the river below!

Price: A. (Concessions; OAP, children).
Facilities: Ⓟ ⎡s⎤ ⎡⎘⎤ ⎡wc⎤
Open: Easter to 31 October, Monday to Friday 9.30am-5pm, weekends 10am-5pm. November to Easter 10am-4.30pm.
Situated: Cromford, south of Matlock.
Nearby: 31, 39, 97, 166.   ☏ (0629) 824297

20. Cusworth Hall Museum (The Museum of South Yorkshire Life) (E3)

Situated in Cusworth Hall, the 18th century mansion of the Wrightson family, the museum illustrates, through both permanent and temporary exhibitions, the everyday life and history of "South Yorkshire folk".

Price: Free.
Facilities: Ⓟ ⎡wc⎤ ♿
Open: Monday to Friday 10am-5pm, Saturday 11am-5pm, Sunday 1pm-5pm.
Situated: Cusworth, north-west of Doncaster.
Nearby: 17, 21, 28, 30.   ☏ (0302) 782342

21. Doncaster Mansion House (E3)

Originally the Doncaster Mayoral residence, and one of only three Civic Mansion Houses in the country. Built around 1750 by James Paine, it has not been used as a Mayor's residence for 150 years, although due to the splendour of the interior it is used occasionally for social and civic functions. Visiting by appointment only.

Situated: High Street, Doncaster.
Nearby: 17, 20, 28, 30.   ☏ (0302) 734019

The Newcomen Beam Engine, Elsecar Heritage Centre.

22. Elsecar Heritage Centre (C4)

Built around 1850, the original Elsecar workshops were the centre of local industry on the Wentworth estate for the engineering enterprises of the Earls Fitzwilliam of nearby Wentworth Woodhouse. In 1988 the local Barnsley Council purchased the workshops and converted them into the Heritage Centre. Displays and activities include the Newcomen Beam Engine, the Bottle Museum, the Hot Metal Press, outdoor exhibitions, craft workshops and "Elsecar People" – a local history exhibition. At the time of writing there are plans to re-open the Fitzwilliam railway station in the centre and run a steam locomotive along a two mile stretch of track alongside the Dove and Dearne canal, complete with genuine 1950's hand-painted carriages. An English Heritage property.

Price: A. (The local history exhibition only).
Facilities: ℗ ◨ [wc] [s]
Open: Daily 8.30am-5.30pm (individual workshops may vary).
Situated: Elsecar, on B6097 off junction 36 of M1.
Nearby: 38, 71, 115, 127.　　　　　☏ (0226) 740203

23. Globe Works Heritage Centre (C5)

Once a cutlery factory, it has now been converted into craft workshops with a permanent display illustrating the development of the Sheffield cutlery industry.

Price: Free.
Facilities: ⬚ ♿ [S]
Open: Monday to Friday 10am-5pm.
Situated: Penistone Road, Sheffield, off A61 north-west of the city centre.
Nearby: 55, 62, 67, 108. ☎ (0742) 822300

24. Graves Art Gallery (C5)

Concentrates on British and European paintings since the 16th century, with works from most of the major periods in the history of art, constituting one of the best collections of water colours in the country. The gallery also houses the Grice collection of ivories.

Price: Free.
Facilities: [WC] ⬚ ♿
Open: Monday to Saturday 10am-5pm.
Situated: Top floor of the Sheffield Central Library.
Nearby: 29, 54, 57, 67. ☎ (0742) 734781

25. Haddon Hall (B7)

Owned and still lived in by the Duke of Rutland, the Hall covers many architectural periods (12th to the 16th centuries), all using the same weathered stone to produce the finest and possibly the most authentic medieval manor house in England, with beautiful rose gardens. Much of it is furnished as it was. Look out for the original kitchens, the banqueting hall and the long minstrel's gallery. There is also a small museum containing items found during restoration work.

Price: B. (Concessions; OAP, children).
Facilities: [WC] ⬚ Ⓟ ♿ (limited)
Open: 1 March to 30 September, Tuesday to Sunday, 11am-6pm. July and August Tuesday to Saturday.
Situated: On A6 between Bakewell and Matlock.
Nearby: 138, 143, 173, 176. ☎ (0629) 812855

Hardwick Hall.

26. Hardwick Hall (D7)

A majestic Elizabethan house built in the late 16th century for
Elizabeth, Countess of Shrewsbury, more commonly known as
Bess of Hardwick, one of the most powerful personalities of her
era. The hall is distinguished for its symmetry – a rare occurrence
in Tudor England – and for the seemingly excessive amount of
windows, hence the saying "Hardwick Hall, more glass than
wall." The interior is lavish and much of it remains in its original
state. Look out for the exquisite needlework, tapestries, and the
elaborate plaster freize. In the shadow of "new" Hardwick Hall
can be seen the ruins of old Hardwick Hall where Bess was born
in 1520. A National Trust property.

Price: B. (Concessions; children (children under 5 free), National
Trust members free).

Facilities: Ⓟ ☕ WC

Open: April to 31 October, Wednesday, Thursday, Saturday, Sunday.

Situated: South-east of Chesterfield, off the A617, near junction 29 M1.

Nearby: 60, 91, 93, 163. ☎ (0246) 850430

Little John's grave, Hathersage church.

27. Hathersage Church (B5)

The parish church of Saint Michael and All Angels is probably best known as the site of Little John's grave, although whether it is the authentic resting place of Robin Hood's lieutenant will always be in dispute. Local legend maintains that Little John lived and died in a cottage which stood near the church until well into the 19th century, and that in the late 18th century the grave was opened and a thigh bone removed belonging to a man in excess of seven feet tall. The greatest benefactors of the church, which dates back to 1381, were the Eyre family, who are commemorated in the most notable brasses in the church. The family was also remembered by Charlotte Bronte in her book *Jane Eyre* (Charlotte stayed at the village vicarage in 1845). Many features of Hathersage can be identified with the village of Morton in her story.

Situated: Hathersage, off the A625 south-west of Sheffield.
Nearby: 41, 99, 140, 181.

28. Hickleton Hall (D3)

Now a Cheshire Home and not open to the public. This former seat of the Earls of Halifax can now only be admired from the nearby A635, however it is worth the drive past. The nearby church (St Wilfreds) is of interest. In the lychgate can be found three human skulls encased in the wall, whose origins and names remain a mystery. The former Earl of Halifax died without revealing their identity.

Situated: Hickleton, on A635 north-west of Doncaster.
Nearby: 20, 35, 36, 96.

The Bessemer Converter.

29. Kelham Island Industrial Museum (C5)

A developing museum which displays a wide range of locally based products along a well-planned trail of industrial sites, both working and redundant, taking the visitor through Sheffield's 300 year old industrial history. Highlights include the huge 1200 HP River Don steam engine, the silver-plated penny farthing bicycle made for the Czar of Russia and the Bessemer Converter. Local craftsmen can be seen at work in the "Little Mesters" workshops.

Price: A. (Concessions; children, OAP, UB40, families).
Facilities: ♿   wc   ▣   Ⓟ
Open: 6 April to 6 December, Monday to Thursday 10am-4pm, Sunday 11am-4pm.
Situated: Kelham Island, Alma Street, Sheffield (city centre).
Nearby: 23, 55, 67, 108.   ☎ (0742) 722106

30. King's Own Yorkshire Light Infantry Regimental Gallery (E3)

Opened in 1987 in the same building as the Doncaster Museum and Art Gallery, it houses the collections, including uniforms, medals and equipment, of the King's Own Yorkshire Light Infantry. Formed in 1755 as the 53rd Regiment of Foot, the Light

Infantry was created in 1988 following the amalgamation of a number of regiments, including some territorials.

Price: Free.
Facilities: ⎡wc⎤ ♿
Open: Monday to Saturday 10am-5pm, Sunday 2pm-5pm.
Situated: Chequer Road, Doncaster city centre.
Nearby: 17, 20, 21, 28.   ☎ (0302) 734293

31. Leawood Pumphouse (C8)

Built by Graham and Co. of Elsecar to pump water from the River Derwent into the Cromford Canal, the building still houses the original fully-operational steam powered beam engine dating back to about 1850. The machine can be seen "in steam" at various times throughout the year. Nearby are the fully restored junction workshops of the Cromford and High Peak Railway. Contact Matlock Tourist Information Centre for further information.

Price: Free.
Situated: Cromford Canal, High Peak Junction, south of Matlock.
Nearby: 19, 39, 97, 166.   ☎ (0629) 82283

32. Magpie Mine (B7)

The buildings that can be seen on the surface constitute Britain's best remaining example of an 18th and 19th century lead mine. Whilst the underground part of the mine is now closed to the public (it ceased working approximately fifty years ago), the surface workings have been renovated to their original state and give an insight into the history of the mine and the lives of those who worked there. Further information is available from the Peak District Mining Museum in Matlock Bath.

Situated: Off B5055 west of Bakewell.
Nearby: 3, 143, 150, 162.   ☎ (0629) 583834

33. Mansfield Museum and Art Gallery (E7)

Opened in 1904, Mansfield Museum was originally housed in a tin shed! Today it houses permanent galleries containing exhibitions of local history and fine and decorative art, as well as tem-

Magpie Mine.

porary exhibitions. Worth seeing is the small but significant collection of 18th century local porcelain.

Price: Free.
Facilities: ⓢ ♿ ⓦⓒ
Open: Monday to Saturday 10am-5pm.
Situated: Leeming Street, Mansfield town centre.
Nearby: 26, 40, 91, 109.   ☎ (0623) 663088

34. Mappin Art Gallery (C5)

Built originally to house John Newton Mappin's gift of Victorian pictures to the city of Sheffield, the gallery now has a varied programme of changing exhibitions, featuring historical, 20th century and contemporary art. In addition to "hands on" workshops led by professional artists, the gallery often presents chamber concerts and recitals to which its elegant interior is well suited.

Price: Free.
Facilities: ♿ ⓦⓒ ⓢ
Open: Tuesday to Saturday 10am-5pm, Sunday 2pm-5pm.
Situated: Weston Park, Sheffield 10.
Nearby: 21, 59, 92, 108.   ☎ (0742) 726281

35. Miners' Memorial Chapel (B4)

To be found in the Conisbrough All Saints' parish church, this small chapel is a permanent memorial to the coal industry and the people of the area who throughout the years have worked in and around the pits. The walls are constructed from firebricks salvaged from closed pits, the ceiling is "cockered", a method used down the mines to support a roof using pit props and wooden beams, and the windows show aspects of mining and its history.

Situated: On A6023 between Mexborough and Conisborough.
Nearby: 17, 28, 114, 137.   ☎ (0709) 862297

36. Monk Bretton Priory (C3)

Founded in 1154 by monks of the Cluniac order from Pontefract, the Priory has throughout the ages been the focus and subject of many disputes, not all of which were resolved peacefully. The monks left in 1538 during the time of the Dissolution and parts of the buildings were dismantled. The property was bought by the Earl of Shrewsbury who converted the prior's house into a private residence. The site was excavated during the 1920s and today considerable remains can be seen, including the gatehouse, the refectory and parts of the 12th century church. An English Heritage property.

Price: A. (Concessions; OAP, UB40, children, groups, English Heritage members free).
Facilities: ℗ wc ♿
Open: 1 April to 30 September daily 10am-6pm, 1 October to 31 March Tuesday to Sunday 10am-4pm.
Situated: Off A633 east of Barnsley town centre.
Nearby: 18, 96, 98, 118.   ☎ (0226) 204089

37. Mr Straw's House (E6)

A perfect example of a suburban semi-detached house with the interiors unchanged since the 1930s. Of special interest are the kitchen and the washroom (untouched for over sixty years!). A National Trust property.

Price: A. (Concessions; children, National Trust members free).
Open: By pre-booked time ticket, April to October, Tuesday to Saturday.
Situated: 5 & 7 Blyth Grove, Worksop town centre.
Nearby: 49, 86, 90, 102.   ☎ (0909) 482380

Monk Bretton Priory.

38. National Bottle Museum (C4)

Situated within the Elsecar Heritage centre, the Museum houses a fascinating collection of antique bottles, jars, ceramics, and packaging from all over the world, illustrating the importance of bottle-making as a local Barnsley industry dating back to the 17th century.

Price: Free.

Facilities: Ⓟ   ⓓ   wc   s

Open: Site open daily 8.30am-5.30pm (groups by prior arrangement).

Situated: Elsecar Heritage centre, off B6097 junction 36 of M1.

Nearby: 22, 71, 115, 127.   ☎ (0226) 745156

39. National Stone Centre (B8)

The story of stone and its usage through the ages, from prehistoric axes to modern-day industry, displaying all its aspects. Based around six disused quarries, there are trails around some of the finest fossil reefs in the country, plus a unique opportunity to pan for gems.

Price: A. (Concessions; OAP, UB40, children).

Facilities: s   ⓓ   Ⓟ   wc   ♿

Open: Easter to October 10am-5pm daily, November to March 10am-4pm.

Situated: Porter Lane, Wirksworth, off B5035 to Ashbourne.

Nearby: 73, 153, 157, 164.   ☎ (0629) 824833

40. Newstead Abbey (E8)

The original priory on this site was founded in 1170, but it was not until it passed into the hands of the family of Lord Byron the poet, that the building was converted into a magnificent residence. The Byron family lived at Newstead until about 1820 when they were forced to sell to pay off debts, unfortunately allowing the Abbey to again fall into a state of disrepair. During the late 19th century the house was rebuilt in its present Gothic style, although parts of the original priory remain. Many of the rooms are much as the poet would have left them with some fine Byron relics, including a collection of pictures. The Abbey grounds are noted for rare trees, shrubs, beautiful lakes and waterfalls.

Price: B. (Concessions; OAP, UB40, under 16's).
Facilities: ▣ ♿ (by arrangement), ⓢ ⧆wc ℗
Open: Abbey: 26 April to 26 September 12pm-5pm. Gardens: Summer 10am-9pm, Winter 10am-dusk.
Situated: Off A60 south of Mansfield.
Nearby: 33, 80, 117, 144. ☎ (0623) 793557

41. North Lees Hall (B5)

Not open to the public, but easily visible from the road. North Lees is a fine example of a late Elizabethan tower house. One of the original seven halls of Hathersage built by Robert Eyre for his seven sons. It is said that the hall made such an impression on Charlotte Bronte during her stay in the village, that she based her description of "Thornfield Hall", in the novel *Jane Eyre*, upon it.

Situated: Hathersage, south-west of Sheffield on A625.
Nearby: 27, 99, 156, 181.

North Lees Hall.

Nostell Priory.

42. Nostell Priory (C2)

Founded in 1120 by an Augustinian order of monks, unfortunately nothing now remains of the original Abbey. The present house, built on the site of the Priory in 1733 by the Winn family, is well worth visiting for its richly decorated state rooms and fine collection of Chippendale furniture. Other highlights include magnificent Brussels tapestries and a remarkable 18th century dolls house. In the surrounding parkland can be found beautiful rose gardens, lakes and the 16th century Wragby church. A National Trust property.

Price: B. (Concessions; children, group bookings).
Facilities: [wc] ♿ [s] ⎅ Ⓟ
Open: April, May, June, September and October Saturday 12pm-5pm, Sunday 11am-5pm. July and August daily (except Friday) 12pm-5pm, Sunday 11am-5pm.
Situated: South-east of Wakefield, off A638.
Nearby: 77, 96, 183.   ☎ (0924) 863892

43. Oakes Park (C5)

Owned and inhabited by the Bagshawe family since 1699, the house is now unfortunately not open to the public, although various fêtes and steam rallies are held in the grounds during the summer. Dating to 1673 it contains many paintings, including family portraits by the famous local artist Sir Francis Chantrey. In the outbuildings are the justice rooms where Sir William Bagshawe, J.P. held court.

Situated: South of Sheffield city centre off the A61.
Nearby: 4, 6, 89, 104.

Padley Chapel.

44. Ollerenshaw Collection (A5)

This privately-owned museum houses one of the finest and largest collections in the world of the locally-mined Blue John stone in the form of vases, urns, columns, and a unique Blue John table top over one metre in diameter. In addition to other gems and minerals on display, there is Royal Crown Derby porcelain and a number of books and prints dating back to 1600.

Price: Free.
Open: Daily.
Situated: The Blue John Craft Centre, Castleton, south-west of Sheffield on the A625.
Facilities: ⬚s
Nearby: 12, 154, 170, 182.   ☎ (0433) 620642

45. Padley Chapel (B6)

Originally the gatehouse to Padley Hall, the remains of which can be seen to the rear of the chapel, the building was not converted to its present use until 1933 (the hall dates from 1400). The first chapel on the site was hidden on the upper floor of the gatehouse, because of the laws of the time the priests could only worship in secret. The remains of Padley Hall are the site of an annual pilgrimage in commemoration of two Catholic priests found hiding there in 1588 and executed for their beliefs.

Open: Sunday and Wednesday after 2pm, or by appointment.
Situated: Behind Grindleford village railway station, off the B6521 south of Sheffield.
Nearby: 99, 128, 140, 141.　　　　　　　　☎ (0433) 630572

46. Peacock Heritage Centre (C6)

Dating from around 1500, the building was "The Peacock" public house until 1973, when a fire in the premises revealed some medieval timber framing. Now all the plaster and tiles have been removed and the whole building restored to its original state. It is believed that it was primarily used as a public hall belonging to one of the medieval guilds of old Chesterfield. It now houses the town Information Centre and a small exhibition room.

Open: Daily 11am-4pm.
Situated: Low Pavement, Chesterfield town centre.
Nearby: 8, 15, 50, 124.　　　　　　　　☎ (0246) 207777

47. Peak District Mining Museum (C8)

The museum offers the visitor the chance to discover the conditions, laws and history that have affected the lives of the Derbyshire lead miners through the ages. There are exhibits on local geology, tools and working methods, plus original working machines. Also on site is the Temple Mine, a disused fluorite and lead ore mine.

Price: A. (Concessions; children, families)
Facilities: ⓟ ⓢ ｗｃ ♿
Open: Daily 11am-4pm (later closing during busy times).
Situated: The Pavilion, Matlock Bath.
Nearby: 19, 106, 190, 192.　　　　　　　　☎ (0629) 583834

Peveril Castle.

48. Peveril Castle (A5)

Built high upon the crags above the village of Castleton, Peveril Castle dominates the local scenery. Dating back to the 11th century, it was given to William Peverel by William the Conqueror. The keep, added 100 years later by Henry II, is still impressive today. An English Heritage property.

Price: A. (Concessions; OAP, UB40, children, groups, English Heritage members free).

Facilities: ⒟ ⓟ

Open: 1 April to 30 September 10am-6pm, 1 October to 31 March Tuesday to Sunday 10am-4pm.

Situated: Castleton, south-west of Sheffield on the A625.

Nearby: 11, 13, 170, 180.   ☎ (0433) 620613

49. Priory Gatehouse (E6)

Standing at the entrance to Worksop's ancient Priory Church, this unique 14th century gatehouse now houses an exhibition gallery and a tea room. Also worth a visit is the nearby Worksop Museum where the Pilgrim Fathers' story is recreated.

Price: Free.

Facilities: ⏍wc⏎ ⏍s⏎

Open: Wednesday to Saturday 10am-5pm, Sunday 2pm-5pm.

Situated: Cheapside, Worksop town centre.

Nearby: 37, 86, 90, 102.   ☎ (0909) 474173

34

Revolution House.

50. Revolution House (C6)

Taking its name from the Revolution of 1688, this building was an alehouse where three local noblemen met to plot the downfall of James II in favour of William of Orange. The fully refurbished cottage, with period furnishings, now houses a programme of displays and exhibitions on local themes. Parties and guided tours by prior booking.

Facilities: wc &. (limited)

Open: Easter to October daily 10am-4pm, November to Easter Saturday and Sunday 10am-4pm.

Situated: Old Whittington, off the B6052 from Chesterfield.

Nearby: 15, 46, 124, 160. ☏ (0246) 453554

51. Roche Abbey (E5)

Founded in 1187 by Cistercian monks, its name derives from the rocky site on which it stands. During the mid-16th century the site was surrended and plundered by the local villagers, to leave only the present ruins. The beauty of Roche Abbey is its positioning. Flanked on either side by white limestone cliffs overgrown by trees and shrubs, it stands in a spacious valley landscaped by Capability Brown. An English Heritage property.

Price: A. (Concessions; OAP, UB40, children, English Heritage members free).

Facilities: wc Ⓟ &

Open: 1 April to 30 September daily, 10am-6pm, 1 October to 31 March weekends only, 10am-4pm.

Situated: South of Maltby, off the A634.

Nearby: 7, 132, 135, 146. ☏ (0709) 812739

Above: *Roche Abbey (see previous page)*. Below *Rockley Furnace, Rockley Engine House*

52. Rockley Engine House (C3)

The engine house built in 1813 is now unfortunately in a state of disrepair but is open to the public. However, nearby can be found Rockley furnace, the oldest of its type still surviving in Europe. Originally producing pig iron, it ceased production in the mid-18th century after over 100 years of manufacture.

Open: All year.
Situated: Rockley Lane, near Worsbrough, off junction 36 M1.
Nearby: 36, 74, 118, 119.

53. Rufford Abbey (E7)

Founded in 1140 by Cistercian monks, the Abbey was used as a place of worship until the mid-14th century when Black Death and poverty ravaged the land. The number of monks living at the Abbey then dwindled and, in 1535 following the Dissolution, Rufford Abbey closed. Taken over by the Earl of Shrewsbury it was converted into a country house and sadly many of the Abbey buildings were pulled down. Fortunately, the refectory and the cellarium (used for storing food and drink) were incorporated into the house and are now open to the public. Outside, the remains of the abbey are clearly marked giving an indication of its original size and structure.

Price: Free, but some special events are charged for.
Facilities: ⒮ ⓦⒸ ⓟ ♿ (wheelchair loan available), ▱
Open: Easter to September daily, 10am-5pm, October to Easter daily, 10am-4pm.
Situated: Ollerton, off A614 near Mansfield.
Nearby: 107, 109, 110, 139. ☎ (0623) 824513

54. Ruskin Gallery (C5)

Exhibits the collection of the famous Victorian artist and antiquarian John Ruskin, who started the museum in 1875. The Guild of St George, the owners of these paintings, were responsible for their movement to the present site. The collection also includes watercolours, manuscripts, photographs and fine books. The Gallery frequently houses other events and workshops.

Price: Free.
Facilities: ⓦⒸ ⒮ ♿ (limited)
Open: Monday to Saturday 10am-5pm.
Situated: Norfolk Street, Sheffield city centre.
Nearby: 24, 29, 133, 134. ☎ (0742) 735299

55. Sheffield Cathedral (C5)

The Cathedral Church of Saints Peter and Paul is the original Sheffield parish church dating back to about 1430, although much of what is seen today is the result of extension and alteration. Inside there are many relics and monuments from the 16th century, fine examples of stained glass windows depicting local scenes and history, the Shrewsbury Chapel monuments and the St George's Chapel for the York and Lancaster Regiment.

Facilities: &

Open: Daily.

Situated: Sheffield city centre.

Nearby: 54, 57, 59, 67.   ☎ (0742) 753434

56. Sheffield City Museum (C5)

Located in the same building as the Mappin Art Gallery, the Museum houses the largest collection of Sheffield plate in the world, plus a notable collection of local and national antiquities, Bronze Age specimens, and a wildlife gallery.

Price: Free.

Facilities: wc &

Open: Tuesday to Saturday 10am-5pm, Sunday 11am-5pm.

Situated: Weston Park, Sheffield 10.

Nearby: 34, 55, 58, 62.   ☎ (0742) 768588

57. Sheffield Heritage Museum (C5)

The Museum features displays from the Sheffield region of trades and crafts plus local customs and folklore. The highlights are the shop and office interiors, including an optician, coffee shop and grocers, faithfully recreated from the early 1900s.

Price: A.

Open: 6 June 2pm-5pm, 3 October 2pm-5pm, 5 December 2pm-5pm. Other times by appointment only.

Situated: 605 Ecclesall Road, Sheffield. (A625).

Nearby: 23, 29, 67, 129.   ☎ (0742) 768555 (X 6296)

Sheffield Manor Turret House.

58. Sheffield Manor (C5)

The remains of Sheffield Manor house stand high above the city in what was once the deer park of the Lords of the Manor of Sheffield. All that is left standing and watertight is the Turret House dating back to 1574, which contains a small exhibition on the history of the Manor, including the imprisonment of Mary, Queen of Scots by the Earl of Shrewsbury.

Price: A.
Facilities: ♿ (limited)
Open: By appointment only.
Situated: Manor Lane, Sheffield 2.
Nearby: 43, 89, 92, 197. ☎ (0742) 768588

59. Shepherd Wheel (C5)

This is not, as its name suggests, an agricultural site, but a former water-powered knife grinding works dating back to the late 18th century. Although the grinding wheel is not fully operational it is the only one of its period to survive in Sheffield, and both it and the interior of the works give a good impression of what life as a "grinder" must have been like.

Price: Free.
Open: Wednesday to Saturday 10am-5pm, Sunday 11am-5pm (4pm in winter).
Situated: Whiteley Woods, near Rustlings Road, Sheffield 10.
Nearby: 55, 57, 197, 198.

60. Stainsby Mill (D7)

The mill at Stainsby was built in 1850 to grind flour for the Hardwick Estate. Restored in 1991 by the National Trust, its water-powered machinery is now in full working order.

Price: A. (Concessions; children).
Facilities: At Hardwick Hall (No 26).
Open: 1 April to 31 October, Wednesday, Thursday, Saturday, Sunday (pm only).
Nearby: 26, 91, 93, 163.

61. Steetley Chapel (E6)

This tiny chapel, found in a small village, is only sixteen metres long and under five metres wide, yet it is probably the finest example of Norman architecture in Derbyshire. No-one is quite sure why such an unremarkable chapel should be decorated to such a high degree of extravagance.

Open: Daily.
Situated: Steetley, off the A57 (near Rhodesia), just west of Worksop.
Nearby: 37, 49, 158, 159.

62. South Yorkshire Fire Museum (C5)

Situated in the old fire/police station, the museum displays fire engines, equipment, uniforms etc of all ages from all around the world.

Price: A. (Concessions; OAP, UB40, children).
Facilities: [wc] &. (limited)
Open: April to December Sundays, 11am-5pm. (other times by prior appointment).
Situated: West Bar, Sheffield city centre.
Nearby: 23, 29, 125, 197. ☎ (0742) 752147

63. Sutton Scarsdale Hall (D7)

Once the grandest 18th century mansion in Derbyshire, now a ruin to be viewed from the exterior only. There are still visible remains of the original 17th century buildings, including the old priory.

Open: Any time (exterior only).
Situated: Near Arkwright Town, off the A632 between Chesterfield and Bolsover.
Nearby: 8, 26, 91, 122.

64. Temple Mine (C8)

A mine worked since 1922 for fluorite, now reconstructed as early 20th century workings. A tour involves not only an insight into mining life underground and the equipment used, but gives an understanding of the local geology which produced the mineral. On the same site as the Peak District Mining Museum.

Price: A. (Concessions; children, families).
Facilities: Ⓟ ⓈＳ ｗｃ
Open: Easter to October daily, 11am-4pm (later closing during busy times).
Situated: Matlock Bath.
Nearby: 47, 106, 190, 192. ☎ (0629) 583834

65. Thorpe Salvin Hall (D5)

A ruined Tudor hall best seen from the nearby road. All that remains of the 16th century house is the south front, however that alone is worth seeing. Built by the local Sandford family, it eventually passed onto the Osbornes who lived there until 1697, since which time it has been empty.

Open: Exterior only, any reasonable time.
Situated: Thorpe Salvin, off the A57 between Sheffield and Worksop.
Nearby: 37, 49, 94, 105.

Thorpe Salvin Hall.

Tideswell church, "The Cathedral of the Peak".

66. Tideswell Church (A6)

"The Cathedral of the Peak", Tideswell church dates back to the 14th century when unfortunately its completion was delayed by the Black Death of 1349. The beauty of this church is in the interior, with lovely stained glass windows and wood carvings, unusual brasses, and a soaring chancel considered to be one of the finest in Derbyshire.

Open: Daily until dusk.
Situated: Tideswell, off the A623 east of Buxton.
Nearby: 88, 101, 123, 172.

67. Turner Museum of Glass (C5)

Houses a permanent display of glass through the ages, most of which was given by Professor W. Turner, the founder of glass technology, who began collecting in 1920 whilst travelling in Europe and America. In addition to pieces by major 20th century glass designers there is also a small Roman collection and a number of 18th century English drinking glasses.

Price: Free.
Facilities: ⌷wc⌷ ♿ (limited)
Open: Monday to Friday 10am-5pm.
Situated: Sir Robert Hadfield building, The University of Sheffield, Mappin Street, Sheffield 10.
Nearby: 1, 4, 34, 59.   ☎ (0742) 768555

68. Untitled Gallery (C5)

Houses one of the largest photographic galleries in the country with many exhibitions, frequently on local themes.

Price: Free..
Facilities: ♿   [S]   ⌨
Open: Monday to Saturday 10am-5.30pm.
Situated: Brown Street, Sheffield city centre.
Nearby: 23, 24, 29, 54.   ☎ (0742) 725947

69. Victoria Jubilee Museum (C3)

First opened in 1884 in a disused cottage on the site of the present building, it became so successful that five years later the new and larger museum was built from materials salvaged from the nearby Cannon Hall estate. This new structure, built to commemorate Queen Victoria's Golden Jubilee, was extended again in 1983. There are exhibits of local history and collections of rocks, fossils, bird eggs and butterflies.

Price: A.
Open: Saturday and Sunday 2pm-5pm.
Situated: Cawthorne, on the A635 west of Barnsley.
Nearby: 82, 83, 183, 189.   ☎ (0226) 790246/791273

70. The Watch House (B5)

A building with a macabre history, the Watch House stands in a small village graveyard on the outskirts of Sheffield. Built in 1784, its sole purpose was as a hiding place to enable people to protect the graveyard from body-snatchers, a pastime which provided the perpetrators with a profitable income by selling the corpses to local doctors and hospitals.

Open: Any reasonable time (exterior only).
Situated: The church of St Nicholas, Upper Bradfield, off the B6077 north-west of Sheffield.
Nearby: 75, 110.

For illustration see following page

The Watch House (see No 70, previous page).

71. Wentworth Woodhouse (C4)

One of Britain's most impressive stately homes and certainly the longest, with a frontage of over 600 feet. Unfortunately the house itself is not open to the public, but is most impressive when viewed from the outside, where it can be seen to be two houses built almost simultaneously by the Wentworth family in the mid-18th century with an obvious scant disregard for cost! The gardens are equally interesting, containing a fine collection of some follies, again all erected by the Wentworth family. Probably the most impressive and certainly the most bizarre is the Needle's Eye, a 48 feet high tapering column with an archway running through its base. The story goes that it was built in order that the 2nd Marquess could prove it was possible to drive a stagecoach through the eye of a needle! Also worth seeing just south of Wentworth village, next to the Garden Centre, are the remains of a 19th century Japanese garden, containing many strange statues and a 19th century bear pit.

Open: Gardens only.
Situated: Wentworth, 5 miles north-west of Rotherham.
Nearby: 22, 115, 127, 137.

The Needle's Eye, Wentworth Woodhouse.

Winster Market House.

72. Winster Market House (B8)

The main building of the village, the market hall dates back to the late 15th century when it was built with an open ground floor on pointed arches. The 17th century upper floor now houses a National Trust information centre. A National Trust property.

Open: 1 April to 31 October daily 11am-5pm.
Situated: Winster, 4 miles west of Matlock.
Nearby: 87, 73, 179, 195.　　　　　　　☎ (033529) 245

73. Wirksworth Heritage Centre (B8)

A former silk and velvet mill, the centre now contains many displays and exhibits on Wirksworth and its history from Roman times to the present. The local custom of well dressing is explained, as are the town's ancient lead mining industry and its link with quarrying. History is well illustrated by recreations of period dwellings and a cavern.

Price: A. (Concessions; children, OAP, families, group bookings).
Facilities: [wc] [s] [&]
Open: Most of the year, telephone for further information.
Situated: Market Place, Wirksworth, off the B5023 south of Matlock.
Nearby: 39, 153, 157, 164.　　　　　　　☎ (0629) 825225

46

74. Worsbrough Mill Museum (C3)

There has been a mill on this site since 1086. The present building, a water-powered corn mill, dates back to about 1625. During the mid-1800s a steam-driven mill was added to meet the demand from an ever increasing population. In 1922 this was scrapped and by 1965 the water mill was redundant and the building derelict. During the 1970s a renovation programme was undertaken and the mill was restored to complete working order with the steam engine being replaced by a rare oil engine. The visitor is now able to wander through the mill and watch flour being ground. Admission by small donation.

Facilities: ℗ ♿ ⅃ s wc
Open: Wednesday to Sunday 10am-5pm. Closed Christmas period.
Situated: Off the A61, junction 36 M1.
Nearby: 36, 52, 118, 119.　　　　　　　　☎ (0226) 774527

75. Wortley Top Forge (C4)

Believed to be the only iron works in Britain still on its original site. Dating back to the 17th century it originally produced iron for the nail industry and later, train axles, before closing in 1910. Now the forge is restored and houses a number of industrial relics, including a blacksmith's shop and a collection of steam engines.

Price: A, (Concessions; children).
Open: Sunday 11am-5pm. Other times by appointment.
Situated: Near Thurgoland, on the A629 south-west of Barnsley.
Nearby: 70, 74, 119, 118.　　　　　　　　☎ (0226) 201848

76. York and Lancaster Regimental Museum (D4)

Found in Rotherham Central Library, the museum displays are designed to show the visitor the history of the Regiment from 1758 until disbandment in 1968. It features uniforms, weapons, illustrations and a unique collection of 1000 medals including 9 Victoria Crosses.

Price: Free.
Facilities: wc ⅃ s ♿
Open: Tuesday to Saturday 10am-5pm.
Situated: Rotherham Central Library.
Nearby: 5, 16, 114, 131.　　　　☎ (0709) 382121 (X3621)

77. Yorkshire Mining Museum (The Caphouse Experience) (B2)

An insight into the mining industry, past and present, with an underground tour where local miners guide the visitor through authentic workings some 450 feet below the surface. Above ground are many diplays, videos and exhibitions on the mining industry, including working models and stories of the various tragedies that have affected the local industry and its people. Has won numerous tourism awards.

Price: B. (Concessions; children, families).
Facilities: ♿   wc   Ⓟ   ⌨   S
Open: Daily 10am-5pm. (Allow 4 hours for a thorough visit).
Situated: West of Wakefield on A642.
Nearby: 69, 82, 83, 183.   ☎ (0924) 848806

COUNTRY PARKS
GARDENS
WILDLIFE ATTRACTIONS

78. Bath House Farm (C7)

Recently landscaped with extensive views over Ashover, the garden contains a wide variety of heathers and mixed borders, a waterfall with pond and stream and a variety of rare trees and shrubs. A member of the National Gardens Scheme.

Price: A. (Children free).
Facilities: 🚻
Open: By appointment June to August.
Situated: Ashover, north of Matlock on A632.
Nearby: 97, 103, 120, 142.   ☎ (0246) 590562

79. Bramley Hall Cottage (C6)

An informal garden with beautiful views containing a wide range of unusual shrubs and clematis, a secret garden, a hydrangea walk and a stream garden. A member of the National Gardens Scheme.

Price: A. (Children free).
Facilities: 🚻
Open: Sundays; June 6, 20 and August 15 (2pm-5pm).
Situated: Chapel Lane, Apperknowle, north of Chesterfield.
Nearby: 50, 112, 124, 160.

80. Butterflies Pleasure Park (E8)

A thirty acre park complete with a tropical house with rainforest atmosphere. Butterflies from all over the world can be seen, along with snakes, lizards, and spiders. Outside is a landscaped park with native flora and fauna. Other attractions include an adventure playground, mini golf and a garden centre.

Price: A. (Concessions; children under four, group bookings).
Facilities: [S] 🚻 Ⓟ &
Open: Daily, 10am-5pm.
Situated: The White Post Centre, Farnsfield, off the A617 east of Mansfield.
Nearby: 53, 107, 117, 144.   ☎ (0623) 882773

49

81. Buxton Pavilion Gardens (A6)

Situated either side of the River Wye, the gardens were developed at the time of Buxton's birth as a spa with money from the 6th and 7th Dukes of Devonshire. The pavilion was built in 1871, with the octagon concert hall added in 1875. The 23 acre gardens contain a play area, and a conservatory restored to its Victorian splendour complete with both native and tropical plants.

Facilities: Ⓟ wc 🚻
Open: All year.
Situated: Buxton town centre.
Nearby: 9, 10, 175, 186.   ☎ (0298) 23114

82. Cannon Hall Country Park (C4)

The house itself is architecturally straightforward, although it does contain an interesting collection of local memorabilia. The 70 acre gardens surrounding the house were landscaped in the 1760's and contain several lakes, walled gardens and a variety of native flora and fauna. There are regular guided walks around the gardens.

Price: Free.
Facilities: wc ⬜ Ⓟ 🚻
Open: All year Tuesday to Saturday.
Situated: On A635 west of Barnsley, near Cawthorne.
Nearby: 69, 83, 183, 189.   ☎ (0226) 790270

83. Cannon Hall Open Farm (C4)

Originally the farm to the whole of the Cannon Hall Estate, Cannon Hall Open Farm, whilst still being a family run working farm, now treats visitors as its main priority. It aims to provide an in-depth, informative and entertaining view of modern day farming. As well as the usual domestic farm animals, the visitor can also see more exotic breeds, such as Vietnamese pot bellied pigs, chipmunks and Anglo Nubian goats.

Price: A. (Concessions; OAP, children, schools, group bookings).
Facilities: s 🚻 (limited), Ⓟ wc
Open: 14 February to 1 November, Tuesday to Saturday 12pm-
4.30pm. Sundays and Bank Holidays 11am-5pm.
Situated: On A635 west of Barnsley, near Cawthorne.
Nearby: 69, 82, 183, 189.   ☎ (0226) 790427

84. Chatsworth Farmyard (B7)

On the same site as the famous stately home, the farm is equally worth a visit. In addition to the ordinary and rarer animals that can be seen there are live farming exhibitions, daily milking displays and a fish farm. Nearby there is an adventure playground. The Chatsworth farm shop can be found in the village of Pilsley (about 2 miles away), selling estate produce.

Price: A. (Concessions; groups).
Facilities: ☕ [S] Ⓟ [WC]
Open: 21 March to 3 October, daily 10.30am-4.30pm.
Situated: Chatsworth Estate, north of Matlock.
Nearby: 14, 126, 138, 167. ☎ (0246) 583139

85. Chestnut Centre (A5)

Founded in 1984 initially to conserve otters and barn owls, the Centre now has breeding enclosures and sanctuaries for otters, owls, falcons and hawks, with on-going programmes for release back into the wild. Visitors follow a trail around the various enclosures with information boards at regular intervals.

Price: B. (Concessions; children, under fives free).
Facilities: [S] [WC] ☕ Ⓟ
Open: March to December, daily 10.30am-5.30pm, January and February weekends.
Situated: On the A625 east of Chapel en le Frith.
Nearby: 154, 168, 170. ☎ (0298) 814099

86. Clumber Park (E6)

A National Trust property consisting of 3800 acres of parkland, including the famous Dukes Avenue bordered along its three mile length entirely by lime trees. The park was created in the early 18th century for the "Queen's use", complete with house and lake. Unfortunately only the lake remains of this original estate, along with a lovely church built during the late 19th century. In addition, there are horse trials, music concerts, sponsored walks and many other events held throughout the year.

Facilities: ♿ [WC] ☕ Ⓟ
Open: All year.
Situated: South-east of Worksop.
Nearby: 102, 110, 113, 139. ☎ (0909) 476592

87. Darley House (B7)

Featured on the B.B.C. "Gardeners World" programme, these gardens were initially landscaped by Sir Joseph Paxton in 1845, but have been restored more recently to include many rare plants and trees. Balustrades and steps separate the upper and lower gardens in which can be found a scale replica of Haddon Hall. A member of the National Gardens Scheme.

Price: A. (Children free).
Facilities: ♿   ▣
Open: By appointment 24 April to 26 September.
Situated: Darley Dale, north of Matlock.
Nearby: 72, 191, 193, 195.   ☎ (0629) 733341

88. Fir Croft (B6)

A plantsman's garden with rockeries, water garden, an extensive collection of alpines and conifers and a small nursery. A member of the National Gardens Scheme. Admission by donation.

Open: Nursery opens every Saturday, Sunday and Monday, March to December. Gardens are open various Sundays, April to June.
Situated: Froggatt Road, Calver, north of Bakewell.
Nearby: 3, 45, 141, 152.

89. Graves Park (C5)

The largest park in Sheffield, providing a wonderful view of the city centre and beyond. It contains the rare breed centre, an unusual sculpture trail dedicated to the locally born sculptor and artist Sir Francis Chantrey and acres of pleasant woodland.

Facilities: ♿   wc   ▣
Open: Daily.
Situated: Norton, off the A61 on the south side of Sheffield.
Nearby: 58, 79, 133, 177.

90. Green Mile (F5)

An unusual garden consisting of eight acres of mixed woodland, rhododendrons, and azaleas bordering onto a lake. There is also a pleasant heather garden and a large display of old-fashioned roses. A member of the National Gardens Scheme.

Price: A. (Concessions; children).
Facilities: &
Open: Sunday 27 June.
Situated: Babworth, 3 miles west of Retford.
Nearby: 102, 121, 130, 171.

91. Hardwick Hall Park (D7)

A 300 acre park with woodland surrounding Hardwick Hall, grazed by herds of longhorn cattle and white-faced sheep. Also worth seeing are the gardens next to the house. Elizabethan in style, most are walled and contain flowers and herbs with lovely grass walks between yew and hornbeam hedges. See also Hardwick Hall (No 26). A National Trust property.

Price: A. (National Trust members free).
Facilities: [wc] (P) (D)
Open: Gardens are open daily 12pm-5.30pm.
Situated: South-east of Chesterfield, off the A617, near junction 29 M1.
Nearby: 26, 60, 93, 163.   ☎ (0246) 850430

92. Heeley City Farm (C5)

Built on reclaimed land, this farm in the city forms an area where domestic and farm animals are kept and country produce grown. Featured on the B.B.C programme "Challenge Anneka". Very popular with children.

Facilities: & (with advanced notice), (D) [wc]
Open: Daily 9am-5pm.
Situated: Richards Road, Heeley, Sheffield 2.
Nearby: 6, 34, 57, 104.   ☎ (0742) 580482

93. Hardstoft Herb Garden (D7)

Opened in 1983, it consists of four gardens each with a different theme, the largest being the mixed herb garden. Also to be seen are the physic garden featuring medicinal plants from around the world, the pot pourri garden and the lavender garden which houses one of the most comprehensive collections in the country. A July or August visit is recommended to catch the garden at its most fragrant.

Price: Free.
Facilities: ♿ [s]
Open: 1 March to 30 September 10am-6pm.
Situated: Hardstoft, off the B6039 near junction 29 M1.
Nearby: 26, 63, 91, 163.   ☎ (0246) 854268

94. Hodsock Priory Gardens (E5)

The 5 acre gardens to a Victorian mansion (not open to the public). Bounded by a dry moat the entrance is through a 16th century gatehouse into a delightfully set garden of mixed borders, roses, mature trees and a small lake. The site itself was mentioned in the Domesday Book. A member of the National Gardens Scheme.

Price: A. (Concessions; children).
Facilities: ⊞ ♿
Open: Sundays and Wednesdays throughout summer, telephone to confirm.
Situated: Off the B6045 between Blyth and Worksop.
Nearby: 90, 102, 121, 171.   ☎ (0909) 591204

95. Hope Gardens (B5)

Different gardens of various types throughout the village, surrounded by beautiful countryside. A member of the National Garden Scheme.

Price: A.
Facilities: (In the village), [wc] Ⓟ ⊞
Open: Sundays in June.
Situated: Hope, west of Sheffield on the A625.
Nearby: 11, 12, 151, 168.

Hodsock Priory gatehouse.

96. Howell Wood Country Park (C3)

Dating back to the 1700s, the wood was planted mainly as a game reserve for the nearby Burntwood Nook, a small country mansion. Today, however, it is open for the general public to explore with various set trails and walks. In addition to the natural scenery there is an unusual ice-house to visit, where the gardeners of Burntwood Nook would store fish caught from the lake, and the hunting lodge.

Facilities: ♿ (on some walks), [wc] Ⓝ
Open: All year.
Situated: Off the B6273 east of Barnsley.
Nearby: 20, 28, 36, 42.

97. Lea Gardens (C8)

Created by John Marsden-Smedley, a woollen manufacturer in the early part of the 20th century, the four acre gardens feature a rare collection of azaleas, rhododendrons, alpines and conifers on a hillside in a delightful woodland setting. A May visit is recommended to see the flowering azaleas and rhododendrons. A member of the National Gardens Scheme.

Price: A. (Concessions; children).
Facilities: Ⓝ Ⓜ ♿
Open: 20 March to 31 July, daily 10am-7pm.
Situated: Lea, south-east of Matlock.
Nearby: 31, 166, 187, 188.

Locke Park.

98. Locke Park (C3)

Donated to the town of Barnsley in 1841 by the wife of Joseph Locke in his memory. This 46 acre park contains not only a statue of Locke (a railway builder) but also a magnificent Italianate tower built in 1877 in memory of Mrs Locke, from where it is possible to gain fine views of the town.

Facilities: wc
Open: All year.
Situated: Barnsley town centre off the A6133.
Nearby: 18, 36, 74, 119.

99. Longshaw Estate (B5)

Owned by the National Trust, the estate consists of 1,600 acres of open moorland and woodland, with wonderful views and varied walking. Above Grindleford Station can be visited an old quarry-winding house from the days when the stone for the Derwent dams was taken from the area. Nearby is the locally renowned "Toads Mouth" rock formation. Guided walks around the estate are available.

Facilities: s ⊞ ⑫ ♿ (limited), wc
Open: All year, visitors centre is open weekends throughout the year.
Situated: Off the A625 south of Sheffield, near Hathersage.
Nearby: 27, 45, 140, 151.   ☎ (0433) 631708

100. Matlock Bath Aquarium (C8)

Built on the site of the original thermal swimming pool, the aquarium houses a number of assorted tanks and pools with both tropical and freshwater fish, some of which can be fed by hand. Also the site of the Hologram Gallery.

Price: A.
Facilities: Nearby wc Ⓟ
Open: Easter to September daily 10am-5.30pm. Winter, weekends only.
Situated: North Parade, Matlock Bath.
Nearby: 190, 191, 192, 193.   ☎ (0629) 583624

101. Millers Dale Nature Reserve (A6)

A site of special scientific interest, the area is managed by Derbyshire Wildlife Trust and is home to many woodland and riverside birds. Once an old quarry, the floor is rich in native plantlife.

Open: All year.
Situated: Near Litton Mill, off the B6049 east of Buxton.
Nearby: 66, 123, 162, 172.

102. Morton Hall (E5)

A medium-sized woodland garden with many different flowering shrubs and trees. A member of the National Gardens Scheme.

Price: A.
Facilities: ⓓ & (part), Ⓟ
Open: Sundays throughout April and May.
Situated: Ranby, west of Retford.
Nearby: 86, 90, 130, 171.

103. Oaks Lane Farm (C7)

An informal garden of just under 1 acre set in beautiful surroundings with herbaceous borders, old fashioned roses and a water feature. A member of the National Gardens Scheme.

Price: A. (Children free).
Facilities: ⓓ & (part)
Open: Early July, telephone for confirmation and appointment.
Situated: Brockhurst, Ashover, off the A632 north of Matlock.
Nearby: 78, 106, 120, 142.   ☎ (0246) 590324

104. Rare Breeds Visitors' Centre (C5)

Surrounded by Graves Park, the centre is the home to a collection of rare breeds of domestic and farm animals.

Price: Free.
Facilities: ♿ (part), wc
Open: Daily.
Situated: Graves Park, Norton, off the A61 on the south side of Sheffield.
Nearby: 6, 43, 58, 89.   ☎ (0742) 582452

105. Renishaw Hall (D6)

Built in 1625 by the Sitwell family who still live in it today, the Hall is not open to the public. The gardens were restored to their original splendour in 1890 by Sir George Sitwell in an Italian style with terraces, ponds and yew hedges. There is also a nature trail.

Price: A. (Concessions; OAP, children).
Facilities: ♿ ▣ s
Open: Sundays and Thursdays in May, June and July.
Situated: On A616 near junction 30 M1.
Nearby: 8, 65, 122, 148.

106. Riber Castle Wildlife Park (C8)

Housed within the grounds of Riber Castle (a magnificent folly built in 1865) is a wildlife collection with the emphasis on rare and endangered species, including the world's most comprehensive lynx collection.

Price: B. (Concessions: OAP, children, groups).
Facilities: wc ▣ ℗ s
Open: Daily from 10am.
Situated: Off the A615 east out of Matlock.
Nearby: 142, 190, 191, 193.   ☎ (0629) 582073

107. Rufford Country Park (E7)

Rufford Abbey stands in many acres of attractive wood and parkland, the centrepiece of which is a lake created in the 18th century, home now to a variety of birds and animals. Closer to the Abbey are more formal gardens with a variety of flora and a number of statues. The craft centre is housed in the old stable block and on the far side of the lake there is the 18th century Rufford Mill which stages changing exhibitions on local life and history. Guided walks can be taken around the Abbey. Car parking charge.

Facilities: [s] [wc] Ⓟ ⅏ ♿
Open: All year. Shop and craft centre daily 11am-5pm.
Situated: Ollerton, off A614 near Mansfield.
Nearby: 53, 109, 110, 139. ☏ (0623) 824153

108. Sheffield Botanical Gardens (C5)

Opened in 1836. Alongside the various borders, woodland areas, flowering shrubs and heath gardens, Sheffield Botanical Gardens has far more to offer than purely plant-life. Just inside the main gates can be seen three glass pavilions designed by Paxton in 1837 based upon Crystal Palace, one of which still houses plants. Further into the gardens is the bearpit, which until the late 19th century was home to two brown bears kept to "entertain" children. Beyond the pit through the gates is the stump of a fossilised tree found during coal mining on the site of the railway station, thought to be 300 million years old.

Open: Daily.
Situated: Clarkehouse Road, to the west of Sheffield city centre.
Nearby: 56, 57, 59, 134.

109. Sherwood Forest Farm Park (E7)

An approved centre for preservation and breeding, the park houses many types of cattle, sheep, pigs, goats and horses, all of which are on show to the public. There are also two small lakes and a water garden, with a large collection of waterfowl. Home to thirty of the rarest breeds of farm animal in Britain.

Price: A. (Concessions; children, OAP, group rates).
Facilities: [s] ⅏ [wc] Ⓟ ♿ (most areas)
Open: Early April to October, daily 10.30am-6pm.
Situated: Off the A6075 between Mansfield and Ollerton.
Nearby: 33, 53, 107, 110. ☏ (0623) 823558

The Major Oak, Sherwood Forest Visitor Centre.

110. Sherwood Forest Visitor Centre (E7)

All that remains of the original Sherwood Forest are 450 acres of silver birch and ancient oaks, the most famous of which is the Major Oak under which Robin Hood and his merry men were said to have hidden. In the Visitor Centre the full story of Robin Hood and Sherwood Forest is told in a walk-through exhibition. Around the centre are various paths to explore the local woods. Car parking charge at weekends.

Facilities: ⓢ ⓦⓒ Ⓟ ⓐ ♿
Open: Daily.
Situated: Edwinstowe, on the A6075 between Mansfield and Ollerton.
Nearby: 33, 53, 107, 109. ☎ (0623) 823202

111. Shipley Country Park (D9)

First mentioned in the Domesday Book as a medieval estate, Shipley grew in the 18th century as a centre for both farming and coalmining. Original houses from that era can still be seen around the park. Industrial relics from Shipley's past have been converted to make the country park: railway lines are now paths, reservoirs are lakes and the old slag heaps have been turned into woodland.

Facilities: ⓢ ⓟ wc ⊡

Open: The park is open all year round, telephone for details of the shop/cafe.

Situated: Off the A608 near junction 26 M1.

Nearby: 40, 185.   ☎ (0773) 719961

112. The Limes (C6)

A large garden with hundreds of daffodils, herbaceous borders, roses, flowering shrubs and rockeries. There are water features, including a large natural pond with ducks and geese.The admission fee also covers a nature trail in the surrounding countryside.

Price: A. (Concessions; children).

Facilities: ♿ ⓟ ⊡

Open: Sundays throughout May, June and July. Evenings by appointment.

Situated: Apperknowle, north of Chesterfield.

Nearby: 50, 79, 124, 160.   ☎ (0246) 412338

113. Thoresby Park (E7)

Thoresby Hall is an impressive Victorian mansion dating back to 1875. Though not open to the public it is surrounded by the largest park in the Dukeries and is almost entirely enclosed by Sherwood Forest. The park often hosts Sunday markets, frequent craft fairs and traction rallies. Cars may drive through the wonderful chestnut avenues in the park and round the ornamental lakes formed by damming the River Meden. On the western side of the lake is a model village built in 1807 and a charming folly called Budby Castle.

Open: All year.

Situated: Off the A614 north of Ollerton.

Nearby: 86, 109, 110, 139.

114. Thrybergh Country Park (D4)

Thrybergh Reservoir, around which the park is situated, was constructed at the end of the 19th century to provide suitable drinking water for Doncaster. The site was bought in 1980 by Rotherham Council for the sum of one pound! Opened three years later to provide a public water sports facility and winter nature reserve, the park is also very important for the conservation of wild life. A bird watching hide is open to the public all year round.

Facilities: ⅙   wc   ℗
Open: All year.
Situated: Off the A630 north-east of Rotherham.
Nearby: 7, 17, 35, 76.   ☏ (0709) 850353

115. Wentworth Castle (C4)

Now a college, Wentworth Castle has South Yorkshire's only Grade One listed garden. Founded in 1672 it was created by Victorian travellers bringing back seeds from their travels around the world, mainly rhododendrons for which it is now famous. Viewing by appointment only.

Situated: South-west of Barnsley, near junction 36 M1.
Nearby: 22, 38, 71, 127.   ☏ (0226) 285426

116. Whistlestop Countryside Centre (C8)

Housed in renovated station buildings, the Derbyshire Wildlife Trust's Countryside Centre features regular wildlife exhibitions and provides the public with information on its various reserves and projects.

Facilities: ℗   wc   s   ⅙
Open: 1 April to 31 October daily 9am-5pm, 1 November to 31 March weekends.
Situated: BR station, Matlock Bath.
Nearby: 87, 106, 192, 193.   ☏ (0629) 580958

117. White Post Modern Farm Centre (E7)

A "hands on" farm centre, visitors are able to experience the life of a modern farmer at first hand. The "wild world of farming" also features fish, snakes and spiders as well as the more conventional domestic animals.

Price: A. (Concessions; OAP, children, under 4's free, school parties).
Facilities: ⒮ ⒟ ⒫ ⦋wc⦌
Open: Monday to Friday 10am-5pm, Weekends 10am-6pm.
Situated: On A614 south of Ollerton.
Nearby: 53, 80, 107, 144.   ☎ (0623) 882977

118. Wigfield Open Farm (C3)

Worked organically, Wigfield Farm is a small mixed farm of about twenty five acres, with arable land for crop cultivation (the wheat grown is ground at nearby Worsborough Mill), and pasture for the animals. The farm has a display of old agricultural machinery and a variety of the rarer breeds of domestic farm animals. Admission by donation.

Facilities: ⒫ ⒮ ⒟ ⦋wc⦌ ♿
Open: Daily 10am-4.30pm.
Situated: On A61, south of Barnsley.
Nearby: 22, 52, 74, 119.   ☎ (0226) 774527

119. Worsbrough Country Park (C3)

Containing the Mill Museum and Wigfield Farm within its boundaries, the park features a fishing reservoir and a wide variety of wildlife, especially birds around the edges of the water. There is also a network of paths around the park and guided walks on a wide range of topics. Admission by donation.

Facilities: ⒫ ⒮ ⒟ ⦋wc⦌ ♿
Open: All year.
Situated: On A61, south of Barnsley.
Nearby: 22, 52, 74, 118.   ☎ (0226) 774527

VILLAGE AND TOWN TRAILS

120. Ashover Village Trail (C7)

Ashover was first mentioned in the Domesday Book although it is thought that the village is much older. Of special interest are the church, which still uses a bell cracked while ringing out news of Napolean's downfall in 1814, and the Crispin Inn which dates back to 1416 when the men of Ashover returned from the Battle of Agincourt, fought on St Crispins day. Guides can be obtained from the Tourist Centre in Chesterfield or the village shop in Ashover.

Situated: Off the A632 north-east of Matlock.
Nearby: 78, 97, 103, 142.   ☎ (0246) 207777

121. Blyth Village (E5)

An old village of great architectural merit, Blyth is situated on the ancient London to York highway. On the village green there is an island on which stands a building (now a private residence), founded by the Hospital of St John in the 12th century for the care of lepers. The parish church was developed from a priory built there in 1088 and contains some of the oldest examples of Norman architectural style in England.

Situated: Off the A1, north-east of Worksop.
Nearby: 94, 132, 135, 171.

122. Bolsover Town Trail (D7)

Bolsover offers an interesting contrast between the modern mining industry of the 20th century and the history of yester-year in the shape of the 17th century castle and the parish church which dates back to the 13th century. Guides can be obtained from the Tourist Centre in Chesterfield or the Bolsover Civic Society.

Situated: On the A632, east of Chesterfield.
Nearby: 8, 15, 26, 63.   ☎ (0246) 207777

123. Buxton History Trails (A6)

Although there is evidence of habitation around Buxton in the time of the cave dwellers, the town really developed in Roman times as a spa built around St Ann's well. It was during the 18th century however that the reputation of the mineral waters turned the original settlement into a bustling spa town. It was then that Buxton's most elegant buildings were constructed, most notably the Crescent in the centre of the town, for the 5th Duke of Devonshire. Other buildings worth visiting are the Opera House, the Assembly Rooms, the Devonshire Royal Hospital (once the Great Stables) and the Pavilion Gardens. Guides can be obtained from the Buxton Tourist Information Centre.

Nearby: 9, 10, 81, 175.   ☎ (0298) 25106

124. Chesterfield Town Trail (C6)

Chesterfield is a bustling market town with origins as far back as the 2nd century, as is illustrated by many of the ancient street names – The Shambles, Packer's Row, Glumangate and Knifesmithgate. The present day Chesterfield, however, owes more to the Railway pioneer George Stephenson, who lived in the town during the construction of the North Midland Railway, which in turn led to coal and ironstone mining in the area. The historic trail incorporates the open-air market, The Shambles, Queen's Park and the famous crooked spire. Guides can be obtained from Chesterfield Tourist Information Centre.

Nearby: 5, 15, 50, 79.   ☎ (0246) 207777

125. East End History Trail (C5)

A 5 mile walk along the towpath of the Sheffield Navigaton Canal, from the heart of the city at the newly renovated canal basin as far as Tinsley Locks in the industrial east end of the city. Along the way are many reminders of the city's industrial heritage. Guides can be obtained from the Sheffield Tourist Information Centre.

Nearby: 129, 177, 197, 198.   ☎ (0742) 734671

Edensor church.

126. Edensor Village (B7)

Designed by the architect J. Robertson with Joseph Paxton as planner (then head gardener at Chatsworth), Edensor is a unique village. It was moved from its original site on the other side of the road on an aristocratic whim of the 6th Duke of Devonshire in about 1840. Set in what was a private park it is a model village, mixing many styles and tastes. Look out for a mock Swiss chalet, a Tudor chimney and Italian windows amongst other oddities.

Situated: On Chatsworth Estate, north of Matlock on the B6012.
Nearby: 14, 84, 152, 167.

127. Elsecar to Wentworth Walk (C4)

The Elsecar/Wentworth area is steeped in both social and industrial history, from the 12th century origins of the Wentworth estate up to the 18th and 19th century development of Elsecar into a coal and iron making community. Starting and finishing in Elsecar, in addition to providing an insight into local history, the walk also provides fine views of the surrounding countryside and some of the unusual buildings en route, such as the amazing follies at Wentworth Woodhouse and the Newcomen Beam Engine in the Elsecar Heritage Centre. Elsecar itself is now a conservation area and many of its buildings are listed as of special architectural interest. Guides can be obtained from Barnsley Tourist Information Centre.

Situated: Elsecar, on the B6097 off junction 36 M1.
Nearby: 22, 38, 71, 115. ☎ (0226) 206757

128. Eyam Village (B6)

Made famous as the "plague village", Eyam's notoriety dates from about 1665 when the germs of the bubonic plague arrived from London in a box of cloth sent to the village tailor. Within a year three quarters of the villagers had died and it was only by voluntarily isolating themselves that they prevented the disease from spreading. Reminders and information of the plague can be seen throughout Eyam, including the plague cottages (where it started), Mompessons Well (where the villagers picked up supplies from the "outside world"), Cucklet Dell (where church services were held during the outbreak) and the Riley family graves. In and around Eyam village are several other places worth visiting: Eyam Hall, a 17th century manor house which acts as a local museum, Wet Withens, a Bronze Age circle of twelve stones on Eyam moor, and the village churchyard which contains an Anglo Saxon cross and a strange sundial from which one can tell the time around the world. Guides can be obtained from the village.

Situated: Off the A623 north-west of Bakewell.
Nearby: 45, 66, 88, 141.

129. Five Weirs Walk (C5)

A five mile walk which explores the east side of the city of Sheffield. Passing through the Lower Don Valley, the former heartland of Sheffield steel-making, it illustrates the city's water-powered past through a series of weirs e.g Brightside weir and Hadfield weir, on the River Don. Guides can be obtained from the Sheffield Tourist Information Centre.

Nearby: 125, 177, 197, 198.

☎ (0742) 734671

130. Retford Heritage Trail (F5)

Retford has a history dating back to the Domesday survey of 1086, although much has happened since – including a great fire which destroyed the town in 1528. During the 18th and 19th centuries both East and West Retford prospered with the arrival of local heavy industry and the railways. Much of the town's architecture is due to these prosperous times. The trail begins and ends in the market place and takes in many of the town's historical sites, including a Russian cannon captured at Sebastopol and the oldest chemist shop in the country still on its original site. Guides are available from Retford Tourist Information Centre.

Situated: East of Worksop on the A620.
Nearby: 86, 90, 121, 171.

☎ (0777) 860780

131. Rotherham Round Walk (D4)

The 25 mile Rotherham Roundwalk passes through the most beautiful areas of Rotherham as well as the more industrial. It starts and ends at All Saints Square in Rotherham, although it is possible to join it anywhere en route as it is well marked by a series of arrows. The walker is taken past Wentworth Woodhouse and its follies, past Boston Castle and around the town boundaries via a series of parks, footpaths and tracks. Guides are available from Rotherham Tourist Information Centre.

Nearby: 5, 16, 137, 147.

☎ (0709) 823611

132. Scrooby Village (E5)

Scrooby is a small village that has acquired renown as the
birthplace of William Brewster, one of the leaders of the Pilgrim
Fathers who sailed aboard the *Mayflower* to America in 1620. It
is thought that he lived in what is now the manor farmhouse
from 1588 to 1608. A similar claim is made for the old village inn,
and a cottage next to the church carries a plaque stating that he
stayed there. The village church attracts many visitors as being
where Brewster and other Pilgrim Fathers once worshipped.

Situated: North of Retford on the A638.
Nearby: 51, 135, 171, 194.

133. Sheffield Round Walk (C5)

Whilst called a round walk, this trail is not totally circular,
beginning in the west end of the city and finishing ten miles
further in the south-east. The walk gives access to the open
spaces and inner city parks in the south of Sheffield. Clearly
signposted, the walker is taken through the woods of Whiteley
and Fulwood past the Shepherd Wheel and Forge Dam, and
then down through the picturesque Whirlow Brook Park and
Limb Valley past Abbeydale Industrial Hamlet. The walk then
passes Beauchief Abbey and on to Graves Park where public
transport is available to the city centre. Whilst this walk only
covers a small area of this vast city, others are to be found in the
more outlying areas of Sheffield such as Loxley, Mosborough,
Stocksbridge and Ecclesfield. Guides to all walks are available
from the Sheffield Tourist Information Centre.

Nearby: 29, 55, 134, 161.   ☏ (0742) 734671

134. Sheffield Walkman Tour (C5)

Using a personal stereo provided by the Tourist Information
Centres, it is possible to explore the city centre on an audio-
guided tour at your leisure. The tape offers sound effects, music
and explanation to re-create the history of Sheffield and its
characters. Personal stereos and tapes are available from Sheffield Tourist Information Centres.

Price: A. (Concessions: OAP, UB40, children, groups).
Available: Monday to Friday, 9.30am-5.15pm. Saturday 9.30am-
4.15pm. Last hire time two hours before closing.
Nearby: 23, 59, 133, 161.   ☏ (0742) 734671

The Butter Cross, Tickhill.

135. Tickhill Village (E4)

Once the site of the most important castle in the north, Tickhill is surrounded by industrial colliery country. The castle was built for Richard, the Lion Heart, but was demolished by Oliver Cromwell, leaving just the gatehouse and some curtain wall. The church of St Mary in the centre of the village is large and impressive, originally dating from the 13th century with later additions. It houses remains of medieval glass and monuments of the 15th to 19th centuries. Also of interest are the Parish Room, a fine timbered building once a hospital in the 15th century, and the Butter Cross in the market place which consists of a dome over eight columns on steps.

Situated: East of Rotherham on the A631.
Nearby: 51, 132, 171, 194.

MARKETS, FAIRS
CRAFT CENTRES

136. Bakewell Market (B7)

Mainly agricultural. Held every Monday, dating back to 1330, Bakewell market is a focal point for the farming community of the Peak district. A market for eggs, butter, pots and pans was formerly held in the market hall (now the National Park Information Centre) in the 17th and 18th centuries. Bakewell Agricultural Show held every August is the most important farming event in the Peak District calendar, as well as being one of the best of its type in the country.

> **Situated:** Bakewell market square, off the A6 between Buxton and Matlock.
> **Nearby:** 2, 3, 25, 178.

137. Barbot Taxidermy Studios (D4)

Graham Teasdale, the owner of the studios, is probably the most renowned commercial taxidermist in the country. He is also an expert model maker, blacksmith, tanner and joiner. In addition to working for museums and preserving family pets, he has also preserved larger animals, even an ostrich! Examples of his work can be seen in Clifton Park Museum, Rotherham. Lectures and demonstrations can be arranged, by appointment.

> **Situated:** Barbot Hall Farm, off the B6089 north of Rotherham.
> **Nearby:** 71, 113, 131, 147. ☎ (0709) 364351

138. Cauldwell Mill (B7)

Built in 1874, the centre is an original water-powered flour mill owned and worked by the Cauldwell family through four generations. It is now run by a charitable trust who aim to preserve the mill, its machinery and its tradition of production. The Mill contains permanent craft workshops, glass blowing, wood turning, antique restoration, ceramics, furniture and pottery. There is also

Cauldwell Mill.

a gallery exhibiting local wares, and guided tours around the mill building can be pre-booked.

Price: A. (Concessions; under 5's free. There is no entrance fee to the workshops).

Facilities: Ⓟ wc ♿ ☏ s

Open: Easter to October 10am-6pm, November to Easter 10am-4.30pm. Weekends only during January and February.

Situated: Rowsley, on the A6 south-east of Bakewell.

Nearby: 25, 173, 176, 178. ☏ (0629) 733185

139. Church Farm Craft Workshops (E7)

Housed in delightfully restored traditional farm buildings, crafts on view include toys, stained glass, wood tuning, brass casting, jewellery and coppersmithing.

Facilities: Ⓟ wc ☏ s

Open: Summer 10am-5pm, winter times vary, telephone for details.

Situated: Edwinstowe, on the A6075 between Mansfield and Ollerton.

Nearby: 53, 107, 109, 110. ☏ (0623) 824033

The Round Building.

140. David Mellor Country Shop (B5)

Built on the site of an old gasometer, hence its name "The Round Building", it was purpose designed and built for the production of the famous David Mellor cutlery, as seen in the Victoria and Albert Museum and the Museum of Modern Art in New York. Praised as a masterpiece of modern architecture and built in local stone, the Round Building received a BBC Design Award as well as an award from the Council for the Protection of Rural England. The shop also stocks a collection of the finest British crafts from jam to pottery. Tours of the factory are possible.

Facilities: [s] (P)
Open: Monday to Saturday 10am-5pm.
Situated: Hathersage, south-west of Sheffield on the A625.
Nearby: 27, 41, 45, 181.   ☎ (0433) 650220

141. Derbyshire Craft Centre (B6)

Boasts the largest selection of crafts in the country, local and national in origin, plus a wide range of gifts and cards. The Egon Ronay recommended eating house is renowned for excellent homebaking.

Facilities: (P) [wc] [s] ♿ (D)
Open: Daily 10am-6pm.
Situated: Calver, off the A623 south-west of Bakewell.
Nearby: 88, 128, 152, 162.   ☎ (0433) 631231

142. Hothouse (C8)

Hothouse is one of Britains leading contemporary glass studios. Visitors are able to gain a close view of glassmakers demonstrating traditional glass blowing skills. Glassmaking is in progress most days, but cannot be guaranteed other than at the demonstrations on Bank Holiday weekends.

Facilities: ⓟ s wc

Open: Monday to Friday 11am-5pm, Easter Sunday 11am-5pm.

Situated: Lumsdale Mill, off the A615 out of Matlock.

Nearby: 78, 106, 116, 120.   ☎ (0629) 580821

143. Lathkill Dale Craft Centre (B7)

Set in beautiful surroundings, the centre is host to a variety of crafts, including timber design, antique clock restoration, glass manufacture and painting.

Facilities: s wc   ⓒ ⓟ

Open: Daily 10am-5pm.

Situated: Manor Farm, Over Haddon, off the B5055 south-west of Bakewell.

Nearby: 25, 150, 176; 178.   ☎ (0629) 812390

144. Longdale Craft Centre (E8)

Designed to recreate an 18th century village complete with shopfronts and paved streets, Longdale is Britain's oldest craft centre. In addition to the traditional crafts produced in the workshops, a glimpse of the past is also available through many of the tools still used. Artists can be seen producing a variety of wares including pottery, stained glass and jewellery. A highly recommended restaurant and craft museum are available on site.

Price: A, museum only. (Concessions; OAP, UB40, children, students, groups).

Facilities: s ⓒ wc ⓟ

Open: Daily 9am-6pm, Longdale Restaurant 9am-6pm (closed Monday evenings).

Situated: Off the A60 south of Mansfield.

Nearby: 33, 40, 80, 117.   ☎ (0623) 794858

145. Longnor Craft Centre (A7)

Originally located in the restored Market Hall to display locally produced country furniture. The idea was soon developed to include the work of other local craftspeople, with the result that although the emphasis is still on wood-based produce the range has widened to include photographs, rugs, lamp shades and other crafts.

Facilities: [wc] &. Ⓟ (in the village), [s]
Open: Daily 10am-5pm. January and February weekends only.
Situated: Longnor, off the A515 south of Buxton.
Nearby: 150, 155, 175, 179.   ☏ (0298) 83587

146. Morthen Craft Workshop (D4)

Based in converted stables on a working farm, the main craft on display is the cutting and polishing of semi-precious stones for showing in their natural state and for jewellery. Other crafts can be seen, including floral art, ceramics and wine making. Demonstrations and craft weekends can be organised.

Facilities: Ⓟ [wc] [s] ⓛ
Open: Most days, telephone for confirmation.
Situated: Morthen Lane, Wickersley, off the A631 east of Rotherham.
Nearby: 7, 13, 147, 177.   ☏ (0709) 547346

147. Pear Tree Pottery (E5)

Housed in an old chapel, all pottery displayed, from coffee mugs to vases, is hand-made on a traditional wheel. The potters can be seen at work most of the time, however special demonstrations are available on request. This is one of many traditional potteries in the area.

Facilities: Ⓟ [s]
Open: Daily, telephone for confirmation.
Situated: Firbeck Lane, Dinnington, off the A57 west of Worksop.
Nearby: 7, 13, 177, 146.   ☏ (0909) 564788

Ridgeway Cottage Industry Centre.

148. Ridgeway Cottage Industry Centre (D5)

Contained in a restored 17th century farm with many of the
original features still intact. The centre houses a wide range of
crafts including a blacksmith, a silversmith, a chocolatier, a
candlemaker and a saddler.

Facilities: [wc] ⌨ Ⓟ ♿ [s]

Open: Daily except Monday 10.30am-5pm.

Situated: Kent House Farm, Ridgeway, off the A616 south-east of
Sheffield.

Nearby: 50, 79, 105, 112.   ☎ (0246) 231111 x2449

OUTDOOR PURSUITS
COUNTRY WALKS AND TRAILS

149. Alport Castles (A4)

Situated above the picturesque Upper Derwent Valley is this spectacular land slip site, one of the largest in Britain. A totally natural phenomenon resembling a line of ruined castles, it is one of the few sites in the land where one can actually see and hear erosion taking place as the sandstone slides over the softer shale base.

Situated: Off the A57 Snake Pass, above Hagg Farm Youth Hostel.
Nearby: 168, 169.

150. Arbor Low (A7)

Dating back to about 2,000 BC (Late Neolithic/Early Bronze Age), Derbyshire's most ancient monument sits on the limestone uplands of the White Peak, surrounded by hilltops each surmounted by its own low (burial ground). It consists of about sixty prostrate stones (no-one is sure if they ever stood upright) encircled by a six foot high bank, and is closely associated with the round barrow of Gib Hill, a conical tumulus of slightly later date in the nearby field. It is considered to be a fine example of a henge monument. An English Heritage Property.

Price: A.
Open: All year.
Situated: Upper Oldhams Farm, Monyash, west of Bakewell.
Nearby: 143, 145, 176, 178.

151. Bagshawe Cavern (B5)

A large cavern discovered by leadminers in 1806, it contains many spectacular and beautiful natural formations. Open by appointment only, the cavern is explored by crawling, wading, and sliding through the chambers and features.

Price: B. (Groups only).
Open: Most of the year. Book in advance.
Situated: Bradwell, south-west of Sheffield off the A625.
Nearby: 44, 66, 95, 174.   ☎ (0433) 620540

152. Baslow Edge (B6)

Looking down over the villages of Calver, Baslow and Curbar, this gritstone edge is popular with walkers and climbers alike, providing them with spectacular views across the central Peak District. In addition to a monument to the Duke of Wellington on the edge above Baslow, a Bronze age stone circle can be found on the edge above Curbar. All around are littered the long discarded millstones manufactured from the gritstone for local industry.

Situated: Above Baslow and district, near Bakewell.
Nearby: 88, 126, 141, 181.

153. Black Rock Walks (B8)

A wooded section of the High Peak Trail surrounded by trees and millstone rock, it retains a feeling of remoteness despite its proximity to the roads and houses. Contains picnic sites. A guide is available from Matlock Tourist Information Centre.

Situated: Cromford, south of Matlock.
Nearby: 19, 39, 73, 188. ☎ (0629) 55082

154. Blue John Cavern (A5)

Here the unusual Blue John stone, unique to this particular hillside, can be seen in its natural setting from where it has been mined for centuries. Visitors are guided through the cavern on paved footpaths to view not only the stone but also wonderful natural rock formations, a display of old mining tools and the first known workings of Blue John by Romans 2000 years ago.

Price: B. (Concessions; children (under 5 free), OAP, families).
Facilities: ⒮ ⓟ ⓦⓒ ⒠
Open: Daily, Easter to December 9.30am-5.30pm. Telephone for winter hours.
Situated: Castleton, south-west of Sheffield on the A625.
Nearby: 44, 174, 180, 182. ☎ (0433) 620638

155. Buxton Country Park (A6)

Situated amidst 100 acres of woodland planted in 1820 to hide quarrying and lime-burning activity. Within the park can be found Poole Cavern and Solomon's Temple, a 19th century folly, built on the site of a Neolithic burial mound, to honour Solomon Mycock who permitted excavation of the barrow on his land. The visitors' centre houses many of the artefacts revealed by the 1983 archaeological dig on the site. Guides are available from the Poole Cavern gift shop.

    Open: All year.
    Situated: Buxton.
    Nearby: 9, 10, 81, 186.

156. Carl Wark Hill Fort (B5)

Thought to date back originally to the Iron Age, although some argue that its defence structure is more akin to the post Roman period, Carl Wark is a well-preserved example of the forts of its type. Built over a two acre site, scattered with boulders and rocky outcrops, one rampart still stands to a height of ten feet and gates can be seen in the eastern side.

    Situated: Above Hathersage, off the A625 south-west of Sheffield.
    Nearby: 27, 41, 99, 181.

Carl Wark hill fort.

157. Carsington Water (B8)

One of Britain's most important birdlife sites, Carsington hosts a wide variety of events, exhibitions and lectures throughout the year on local flora and fauna and history. Physical activities include cycling (there is a hire centre), horse riding, water sports and guided walks. There is a visitors' centre by the reservoir for further information.

Facilities: ⓟ ♿ ⓓ |wc| |s|
Open: 1 April to 31 October 10am-6pm (weekends until 8pm).
November to 31 March 10am-4pm (weekends until 5pm).
Situated: On the B5035 between Ashbourne and Wirksworth.
Nearby: 39, 73, 164, 179.   ☏ (0629) 85696

158. Creswell Archaeological Way (D7)

Beginning at the "Meden Valley Trail" car park near Pleasley and ending at Whitwell, the Creswell Archaeological Way has been devised to assist visitors to explore the countryside on the borders of Derbyshire, Nottinghamshire and South Yorkshire. Thirteen miles in length, it guides the visitor past evidence of human activity through the ages, from relics of the Stone Age to the relatively more modern steam railways of the 19th century. Guides can be obtained from either Matlock or Chesterfield Tourist Information Centres.

Situated: Off the A617, on the B6407 north of Mansfield.
Nearby: 8, 49, 86, 159.   ☏ (0623) 742525

159. Creswell Crags (E6)

At the foot of a gorge surrounding a small lake are the 26 caves that once sheltered the Neanderthal man on hunting trips. Evidence has been found of remains of hyena, wolf, brown bear and woolly mammoth, plus primitive tools and weapons dating back over seventy thousand years. The visitors' centre houses exhibitions and an audio-visual display detailing the cave's ancient history.

Price: A. (Telephone in advance for cave tours).
Facilities: ⓟ |wc| |s|
Open: February to October 10.30am-4.30pm, November to January Sundays only.
Situated: Creswell, off the A60 between Mansfield and Worksop.
Nearby: 8, 49, 86, 158.   ☏ (0909) 720378

160. Cuckoo Way (C6)

Chesterfield Canal is a product of the Industrial Revolution, its initial purpose being to transport coal to new markets. Opened in 1777, the canal was a marvellous feat of engineering with the country's longest canal tunnel at Norwood and one of the earliest examples of a staircase lock at Thorpe Salvin. The towpath alongside the 46 mile long canal was named after the vessels which used it (cuckoos), in turn probably named after a hill beneath which the canal runs. Various sections of the path can be attempted, providing not only an insight into local industrial history, but also local wildlife. Further information can be obtained from Chesterfield Tourist Information.

Nearby: 15, 46, 50, 124. ☏ (0246) 207777

161. Dore Stone (C5)

Standing on the village green, the Dore Stone commemorates the unification on this spot in 829 of the Saxon kingdoms of Northumberland, Wessex and Mercia under Ecgbert of Wessex who became the first overall King of England. In July, the Derbyshire tradition of well dressing can be observed at the nearby Peace Well, evidence of the fact that until recently Dore was in Derbyshire and not Yorkshire.

Situated: Dore, off the A625 on the western outskirts of Sheffield.
Nearby: 1, 4, 99, 133.

The Dore Stone.

81

162. Fin Cop (B7)

Situated high up on an impressive moorland escarpment, Fin Cop is an Iron Age hill-fort of about ten acres. The site has well preserved defences including a gate cutting off the headland from the south-east and two barrows.

Situated: Above Ashford in the Water, to the west of Bakewell.
Nearby: 32, 101, 136, 172.

163. Five Pits Trail (D8)

Follows 7 miles of former railway lines between Grassmoor and Tibshelf passing through the Grassmoor Country Park. Suitable for cyclists, walkers and horse riders, there is also a signposted nature trail. Contains picnic sites. Guides are available from Chesterfield Tourist Information Centre.

Nearby: 26, 60, 91, 93.   ☎ (0246) 866960

164. Good Luck Mine (B8)

Situated on the Via Gellia, the Centre is a working example of a 19th century lead mine complete with underground lead mining museum and working surface layout.

Price: A. (Concessions; children under 14).
Facilities: Ⓟ wc
Open: Easter to September, first Sunday in the month 11am-4pm. Advanced booking is essential.
Situated: Via Gellia, Cromford, south of Matlock.
Nearby: 19, 31, 157, 179.   ☎ (0246) 272375

165. Hatfield Marina (F3)

A man-made lake formed from old sand and gravel pits with landscaped surroundings, the marina is now a major centre for both water sports and wildlife. Courses and activities are available on a wide range of subjects from the visitors centre.

Facilities: Ⓟ Ⓓ wc
Open: All year.
Situated: Between Doncaster and Thorne on the A18.
Nearby: 21, 30, 196.   ☎ (0302) 841572

166. High Peak Trail (C8-A6)

A 17 mile long track on the original bed of the High Peak railway line from the Cromford canal basin to Dowlow, near Buxton. Used extensively by walkers, horse riders and cyclists, with a series of car parks and picnic sites. Cycle hire centres are at Parsley Hay and Middleton Top. Guides are available from Buxton and Matlock Tourist Information Centres.

Nearby: 19, 31, 153, 188.   ☎ (0629) 55082 / (0298) 25106

167. Hob Hurst's House (B7)

A Bronze Age barrow surrounded by a square ditch and bank, with a marvellous view overlooking Chatsworth House. Several other cairns and burial monuments are to be seen on the moorland surrounding. Its odd name derives from the local belief in a mischievous wood elf, "Hob i'th Hirst" who is said to inhabit woods, tumuli and other dark, lonely places.

Situated: Near Beeley, off the A6 south-east of Bakewell.
Nearby: 14, 84, 126, 138.

168. Kinder Scout (A5)

A bleak moorland plateau at the summit of the Peak National Park, Kinder Scout derives its name from the Saxon "Kyndwr Scut", meaning "water over the edge" an apt description of the area, especially after heavy rain, although it may have referred solely to the spectacular Kinder Downfall, a 100 feet high waterfall. Possessing spectacular rock scenery, Kinder is also famous for the "mass trespass" of 1932, when 600 ramblers, defending their right to roam the nation's moorlands, confronted the local landowners and gamekeepers, whose aim was to keep the hills out of bounds to the public. Fortunately access agreements were reached and the picturesque moorland is now open for the public to explore, except during the grouse shooting season.

Situated: Above Edale village, off the A625 west of Sheffield.
Nearby: 149, 169.   ☎ (0433) 670207

169. Ladybower and Derwent Reservoirs (B5)

Built to satisfy the needs of growing cities in the Midlands and South Yorkshire, the first of Derbyshire's great dams, Howden and Derwent, were constructed without the loss of many buildings. However when Ladybower was built in 1945 this was not the case. The flooding of the lower Derwent valley resulted in the loss of two villages, Ashopton and Derwent, and when water levels are low it is still possible to see outlines of buildings and walls. Parts of the village of Derwent survived the flooding, including the old school which can be seen by the road towards the Fairholmes car park at the northern end of the Derwent Reservoir. The dams were used as a practice area for the famous "bouncing bombs" of the Dambuster Raids, due to their close resemblance to the intended targets .

Facilities: ℗
Situated: Near Bamford, by the A57 west of Sheffield.
Nearby: 149, 168, 181.

170. Mam Tor (A5)

Known as the "shivering mountain", Mam Tor is aptly named. Landslips are still a regular occurrence and all attempts to build a road across its face have failed. The movement is caused by the unstable make-up of sandstone on shale. Unfortunately the Iron Age hill fort which stood up on the plateau has also been a victim of its instability, but archaeological digs within the remaining earthworks have revealed a once sizeable settlement. From the summit there are wonderful panoramic views of the Derbyshire countryside, including the adjacent Winnats Pass, thought to be a collapsed cave system from the time when the area was a lagoon, completely covered by water.

Situated: Castleton, on the A625 south-west of Sheffield.
Nearby: 48, 170, 180, 182.

Mam Tor.

171. Mayflower Trail (F5)

The Mayflower Trail leads the visitor around the historic sites of Pilgrim Fathers country, beginning and ending in Babworth near Retford. Along the forty mile tour can be seen the churches, country houses and villages that influenced these religious travellers. Of note along the way are the Manor House at Scrooby where William Brewster, one of the Pilgrim Fathers who travelled aboard the *Mayflower*, lived, Gainsborough Old Hall, one of the most complete timber framed medieval houses still standing in the country, and the churches at Austerfield and Babworth. Guides are available from Worksop Tourist Information Centre.

Situated: Babworth, near Retford.
Nearby: 102, 121, 130, 132.   ☏ (0909) 501148

172. Monsal Trail (B7)

Passing through areas of both great beauty and scientific interest in the heart of the Peak District, the trail follows the old Buxton to Matlock section of the Midland Railway. A wonderful view of the entire area can be obtained from Monsal Head across Coombs viaduct, before wandering alongside the River Wye in the valley bottom. For nature lovers part of the dale has been designated a nature reserve, whilst for the more energetic there is a cycle hire centre nearby and two restored 18th century lime kilns in Millers Dale to explore. Guides are available from Bakewell Tourist Information Centre.

Situated: Coombs Viaduct, 1 mile south-east of Bakewell.

Nearby: 32, 66, 101, 162.   ☎ (0629) 813227

173. Nine Ladies Stone Circle (B7)

A Bronze Age stone circle some fifty feet across, the nine standing stones vary in height, although the tallest is a mere 39 inches. Legend has it that these are the burial posts to the graves of nine ladies of Haddon who, whilst struck down with the plague, danced on the moors. Their fiddler's stone can be seen nearby.

Situated: Stanton in the Peak, Birchover, off the A6 north-west of Matlock.

Nearby: 25, 138, 176, 178.

Nine Ladies stone circle.

174. Peak Cavern (A5)

The largest natural cavern in Derbyshire, Peak Cavern is reached through the picturesque Peak Gorge and overlooked by the equally impressive Peveril Castle. Perhaps the .most amazing feature of this enormous cave is that until the mid-19th century people actually lived inside its entrance, in small cottages carved in the rock, complete with underground pub ! The main industry of the cave-dwellers was rope-making, a craft continued up to relatively recent times. Inside the cave are various chambers: The Devil's Hole, Styx and Pluto's Dining Room- reflections of earlier beliefs that the cavern was the entrance to the underworld.

Price: A. (Concessions; OAP, children).
Facilities: ⓢ other facilities in the village
Open: 11 April to 25 October, daily (except Mondays in March to May and September and October), 10am-5pm.
Situated: Castleton, on the A625 south-west of Sheffield.
Nearby: 12, 154, 180, 182. ☎ (0433) 620285

175. Pooles Cavern (A6)

Named after the 15th century outlaw, Poole. Evidence has been found throughout the cave system suggesting that it has been used as a shelter since the Neolithic period (New Stone Age), with relics also from the times of the Romans and the Celts. A large cavern, its rock formations, stalactites and stalagmites are its most impressive features. A visitors' centre displays artefacts from the 1983 archaeological dig in the cavern.

Price: B. (Concessions; OAP, children, students, group bookings).
Facilities: ⓢ ⓒ ♿ ⓦⓒ ⓟ
Open: Easter to November, 10am-5pm. (Closed Wednesdays in April, May, October) Open all year round to group bookings.
Situated: Green Lane, Buxton. (In Buxton Country Park).
Nearby: 9, 10, 81, 186. ☎ (0298) 26978

176. Robin Hood's Stride (B7)

One of many rock formations of interest in the Birchover area, this particular formation consists of two upright stone pillars each about 18 feet in height and 70 feet apart. Their sheer size makes them an impressive landmark and also gives them their alternative name of Mock Beggar's Hall owing to their similarity to the twin towers of a medieval manor house. There is much evidence of man's activity, the area was probably inhabited during Roman times, and the summit is reached by a roadway possibly dating back to that period. Near Robin Hood's stride can be found numerous rocks with artificial markings on them, further evidence of the belief that the village and surrounding regions were the site of Druidical ceremonies during the period following the Celts about 500 BC.

Situated: Birchover, off the A6 north-west of Matlock.
Nearby: 25, 138, 173, 178.

177. Rother Valley Country Park (D5)

Created from 750 acres of old open-cast mine workings, the wood and parkland cater for a variety of activities, both on land and on the three man-made lakes. A network of paths allows the visitor to explore the area and the native flora and fauna. Watersports are available from the lake-side centre, adjacent to which is Bedgreave Mill, an early-17th century grain mill now converted into the visitors' centre. The restored mill houses displays and information on the history of the buildings and the surrounding region, as well as on the many aspects of the park itself. Nearby is the craft centre where local craftsmen can be seen at work. All activities are booked and paid for through the visitors' centre.

Facilities: $\boxed{\text{S}}$ $\textcircled{P}$ $\textcircled{D}$ $\boxed{\text{WC}}$ &. (limited)
Open: All year. Visitors centre 8.30am to dusk.
Situated: Off the A618 near junction 31 M1.
Nearby: 13, 65, 105, 148. ☎ (0742) 471452

178. Rowtor Rocks (B7)

Perhaps the most interesting rock formation in an area containing many fascinating natural features, these huge gritstone blocks are well over 60 feet high and 200 feet long. Amongst the boulders and "rocking stones", which look as though they may fall at any time, are many carvings, markings, passages and caves. Some of these can be attributed to the Reverend Thomas Eyre (died 1717) who used this outcrop as a place to prepare his sermons, some are just a product of man's "vandalism" through the ages. The remainder have a far more intriguing history. There is much evidence to suggest that the Rowtor Rocks were the site of ancient Druidical ceremonies, including human imprisonment and sacrifice!

> **Situated:** Behind the Druids Inn, Birchover, off the A6 north-west of Matlock.
>
> **Nearby:** 25, 138, 173, 176.

179. Roystone Grange Archaeological Trail (B8)

Approximately 4 miles long, the trail begins at Minninglow – the first of a number of archaeological sites en route, where can be found a chambered tomb, one of the most impressive of Derbyshire's remaining prehistoric burial sites. Also to be seen are the Bronze Age barrow at Royston, Roman farm and field systems, medieval grange buildings and the 19th century remains of the High Peak railway. Guides are available from the Bakewell Tourist Information Centre.

> **Situated:** Begins at the Minninglow carpark, off the A5012 west of Matlock.
>
> **Nearby:** 32, 72, 157. ☏ (0629) 813227

180. Speedwell Cavern (A5)

A unique experience, Speedwell is not actually a natural cavern but a flooded 18th century lead-mine explored by boat. The passage itself was carved out by hand to reach the ore, which was then transported to the surface by the canals down which today's visitor is ferried. At the end of the tour is the fascinating "bottomless pit", down which it is reported 40,000 tons of waste rock from the mining was tipped without altering the water level.

> **Price:** B. (Concessions; children).
>
> **Facilities:** wc Ⓟ s ♿
>
> **Open:** Daily from 9.30am.
>
> **Situated:** Castleton, on the A625 west of Sheffield.
>
> **Nearby:** 11, 154, 174, 182. ☏ (0433) 620512

Stanage Edge.

181. Stanage Edge (B5)

The highest section of gritstone edge in the east of the Dark Peak. Stanage is famous amongst climbers for its diversity of routes, and in fact it was on this four-mile wall of rock that the sport was first practised in the 1890's. Littered with abandoned millstones, relics of former local industry, the Edge is also associated with the outlaw Robin Hood, who supposedly hid from his enemies in a cave still surviving halfway up the cragface. There are wonderful views over the village of Hathersage and the surrounding countryside.

Situated: Above Hathersage, west of Sheffield.
Nearby: 27, 41, 99, 169.

182. Treak Cliff Cavern (A5)

Containing the largest workable deposits of the local Blue John stone, Treak Cliff cavern is mostly natural, other than the entrance tunnel by which it is reached. Discovered in the 1700s by local miners, the Old Series of chambers contains some fine fossils and the world's richest Blue John vein. The New Series, discovered in 1926 completely by accident, is more beautiful with colourful rocks and amazing stalactite formations.

Price: B. (Concessions; children, students, YHA members, OAP).
Facilities: ⊡ ℗ wc s
Open: Daily. Summer 9.30am-5.30pm, Winter 9.30am-4pm.
Situated: Castleton, on the A625 west of Sheffield.
Nearby: 44, 154, 174, 180.　　　　　　　　☎ (0433) 620571

183. Yorkshire Sculpture Park (C2)

Situated in beautiful 18th century parkland, the centre displays three dimensional sculpture work by contemporary artists, both local and national. The permanent exhibits include works by Henry Moore, Emile Bourdelle and the Access Trail by Don Rankin, a sensory trail particularly planned for disabled visitors. Often referred to as the gallery without walls, the Park also has an ever changing programme of temporary exhibitions as well as lectures, weekend events and regular guided tours around the Bretton Estate. Admission to the park is free, however a small charge is levied for the courses.

Facilities: s ⊡ wc ℗ ♿
Open: All year, Summer 11am-6pm, Winter 11am-4pm.
Situated: Bretton Hall, Wakefield. Junction 38 M1.
Nearby: 69, 77, 82, 189.　　　　　　　　☎ (0924) 830302

Yorkshire Sculpture Park.

THEME PARKS
RAIL AND TRANSPORT
FAMILY FUN

184. Alton Towers (A9)

Great Britain's only world-rated leisure park. Situated in 500 acres on the former estates of the Earls of Shrewsbury and surrounded by magnificent 19th century gardens, the park offers fun for all in the form of 125 "rides", including the world famous corkscrew.

Price: C. (Concessions; under 14's, family and group bookings).
Facilities: Ⓟ 🏧 ⑯ ⑤
Open: Daily, March to November 10am-6pm. Gardens only in Winter.
Situated: Alton, near Ashbourne. ☎ (0538) 702200

185. American Adventure Theme Park (D9)

A "true" theme park based on the legend of the whole American continent with over 100 "rides". There is also a huge indoor playland open during the winter.

Price: C. (Concessions; children, OAP).
Facilities: ⑯ 🏧 ⑷Ⓒ Ⓟ ⑤
Open: March to November from 10am. Telephone for further information. Indoor playland open every weekend November to April.
Situated: Ilkeston, Derbyshire, off the A607.
Nearby: 40, 111. ☎ (0773) 531521

186. Buxton Micrarium (A6)

The first museum of its kind presenting microscopic images from the world of nature, including a snowflake, water fleas and butterfly wings. The images are projected on to large screens with explanations of what the visitor is viewing. It is situated in the old Victorian pumphouse built in 1894 for those undertaking the spa treatment. Alongside is the drinking fountain where it is possible to sample the natural waters.

Price: A. (Concessions; children).
Facilities: ♿ (part), local Ⓟ
Open: March to November, daily 10am-5pm.
Situated: The Crescent, Buxton town centre.
Nearby: 9, 10, 81, 155. ☎ (0298) 78662

187. Crich Tramway Museum (C8)

Built on a site used by George Stephenson to construct a mineral railway, the Museum boasts over 50 tram cars driven by steam, electricity and horse-power collected from all over the world. Unlimited rides are available on a variety of trams along the electric tramway, giving magnificent views over the Derwent valley below. The site also houses a permanent exhibition on the evolution of the tram and its use through the ages.

Price: B. (Concessions; children, OAP, families).
Facilities: Ⓟ [wc] ⓐ [s]
Open: April to October, daily 10am-5pm (weekends until 6.30pm).
Situated: Off the A6, south of Matlock.
Nearby: 31, 97, 167, 193. ☎ (0773) 852565

Crich Tramway Museum.

Middleton Top Engine House, Cromford and High Peak Railway.

188. Cromford and High Peak Railway (C8)

Opened in 1831 to carry goods from the Cromford Canal to Manchester, the disused line is now the High Peak Trail and is used by walkers, cyclists and horse riders. At various points along the trail can be found the old winding houses used to pull the fully-laden trains up the steep inclines. At the top of the steep Middleton incline can be seen the old engine house built in 1829 by the Butterley Company. Its purpose was to haul the fully laden wagons up the slope. Now converted into a visitor centre, it tells the story of the engine house itself and the High Peak Railway. The High Peak Junction workshops have been fully restored to their 19th century condition and now house a variety of models and exhibitions on the old railway and its history. Picnic sites can be found en route.

Price: A, workshops only. (Concessions; children).

Open: Workshops only, 9 April to 31 October 10.30am-5pm. November to Easter, Sundays 10.30am-4.30pm.

Situated: Cromford, south of Matlock.

Nearby: 31, 39, 153, 166.   ☎ (0629) 823204

189. Denby Dale Pie (B3)

Outside "Pie Hall" in the village of Denby is the flower-filled baking dish used for the world's largest pie. The last one, baked in 1988, to celebrate the bicentenary of the first in 1788, contained 3000 kilos of beef, 3000 kilos of potatoes and 700 kilos of onions! Other pies baked include those to celebrate the defeat of Napolean at Waterloo, to commemorate Queen Victoria's Golden Jubilee and to raise funds for a local community centre.

Situated: Denby Dale, west of Barnsley off the A635.
Nearby: 69, 72, 83, 183.

190. Gulliver's Kingdom (C8)

On the hill overlooking Matlock, Gulliver's Kingdom features over 40 themed rides and attractions including Little Switzerland and Western World, craft shops and live entertainment in the form of puppet shows and magicians.

Price: B. (Concessions; groups, OAP).
Facilities: ⓢ ｗｃ ☒ ⓟ ♿ (telephone prior to visit)
Open: 3 April to 12 September, weekends until 31 October. 10.30am-5.30pm.
Situated: Matlock Bath.
Nearby: 106, 116, 191, 192.   ☎ (0629) 57100

191. Heights of Abraham Country Park (C8)

The park is reached by an exciting cable car ride from river level in Matlock Bath up to the 60 acre wooded site. The main attractions are two show caves – the Rutland-Nestus cavern where the "miner's tale" is told by a 17th century lead miner, and the Great Masson cavern where the story of the rocks is brought alive in multivision. In the park, wonderful views can be gained of the surrounding region, and picturesque walks taken around the nature trail and landscaped waterfalls.

Price: B. (Concessions; children (under 5 free), OAP).
Facilities: ☒ ｗｃ ♿ ⓟ ⓢ
Open: Easter to October daily 10am-5pm. Telephone for winter opening.
Situated: Matlock Bath.
Nearby: 100, 116, 191, 192.   ☎ (0629) 582365

192. Matlock Bath Model Railway Museum (C8)

A must for the railway enthusiast, but be sure to telephone first. It houses a fine 7mm model railway, based upon Millers Dale Station and area at the turn of the century, and displays of railway memorabilia. The shop sells a wide selection of railway books both old and new.

Price: Free.
Facilities: &
Open: All year, Tuesday to Thursday 11am-5pm. Telephone before visiting to confirm.
Situated: Temple Road, Matlock Bath.
Nearby: 100, 106, 116, 193.   ☎ (0629) 580797

193. Peak Rail (C8-C7)

Set up by a group of rail enthusiasts in 1975 with the intention of reopening the Buxton to Matlock rail link, it is twenty miles long with many bridges, tunnels and viaducts. Although the line closed in 1968 the forming of Peak Rail has led to the replacement of tracks between Matlock and Darley Dale. A level crossing has been installed, steam locomotives have been refurbished and a temporary platform built to make this small section of line fully operational. The eventual aim being to reach Buxton. Information on the project and details on how to join the Peak Rail Society can be found at Darley Dale and Matlock BR stations.

Situated: Matlock to Darley Dale.
Nearby: 187, 188, 191, 192.   ☎ (0629) 733476

Peak Rail.

194. R.A.F. Finningley (F4)

The host to the largest aerial display in the country every September, Finningley is very much an active R.A.F. base and is not open to the public other than on the Open Day.

Situated: Finningley, on the A614, south-east of Doncaster.
Nearby: 132, 135, 165.

195. Red House Stables (C7)

A working carriage museum, it has an outstanding display of original horse drawn vehicles and equipment, probably one of the best in Britain. The collection has approximately 40 carriages including a Hansom Cab (one of the few still surviving) and other private and commercial vehicles from the past. Kept in beautiful condition, many of the museum's carriages and horses have been used for television work.

Price: A. (Concessions; children, OAP).
Facilities: wc   ♿   ℗
Open: Daily from 10am.
Situated: Darley Dale, off the A6 between Bakewell and Matlock.
Nearby: 72, 87, 173, 193.   ☎ (0629) 733583

Red House Stables Carriage Museum.

196. Sandtoft Transport Museum (F3)

Houses Britain's largest collection of buses and trolleybuses, including a nostalgic ride on an original trolleybus. Run entirely by volunteers, it is only open to the public on certain weekends during the summer. Further information can be obtained from Doncaster Tourist Information.

Situated: Sandtoft, near junction 2 M180.
Nearby: 165. ☎ (0302) 734309

197. Sheffield Bus Museum (C5)

A recently established museum with an ever growing collection. In addition to public transport vehicles of all types and ages it also displays various transport artefacts and memorabilia, including destination boards, old bus timetables and the Sheffield Model Railway Society's layout. Special event days with various themes are held throughout the year.

Price: A.
Facilities: ⌷wc⌷ ♿ (part)
Open: All year, Saturday and Sunday 12pm-4pm.
Situated: Tinsley Tram Sheds, Sheffield Road, Sheffield 9.
Nearby: 13, 125, 129, 198. ☎ (0742) 553010

198. South Yorkshire Steam Railway (C5)

A collection of over 35 locomotives, carriages and wagons paying homage to Sheffield, the city that made the steel to build railway lines and steam locomotives all over the world. Plans are also afoot to open small local sections of line on which some of the old engines will run.

Price: A, includes three month membership of the society. (Concessions; children).
Open: All year, Saturday and Sunday 11am-4pm.
Situated: Barrow Road, Meadowbank, Sheffield 9.
Nearby: 13, 62, 129, 197. ☎ (0742) 424405

REGIONAL DIARY

JANUARY
Haxey Hood Game.
Haxey, near Doncaster.
(Always on Jan 6th).

FEBRUARY
Ashbourne Football (Shrove Tuesday). Ashbourne.

MARCH
Abbeydale Industrial Hamlet, Working Days. Sheffield.
Flour Milling, Caudwell Mill. Rowsley, near Matlock. (monthly)

APRIL
Wellington re-enactment, Bolsover Castle.
Chesterfield Easter Market.
Flagg Point to Point Races, Flagg Moor, near Buxton.
Retford Easter Market.

MAY
Ashford in the Water Well Dressing, near Bakewell.
Bamford Sheepdog Trials.
Medieval Entertainment, Bolsover Castle.
Buxton Annual Brass Band Festival.
Castleton Garland Ceremony.
Chatsworth Angling Fair.
Clumber Park Horse Trials.
Dambusters Anniversary, 617 Squadron, Ladybower Reservoir.
Derbyshire Steam Fair, Hartington Moor, near Buxton.
Monyash Well Dressing.
Winster Market Fair.
Wirksworth Well Dressing.

JUNE
Abbeydale Industrial Hamlet, Working Days.
Bakewell Well Dressing, Carnival and Raft Race.
Falconry Displays, Bolsover Castle.

Chatsworth Obstacle Race.
Clumber Park Show.
Litton Well Dressing.
Rowsley Well Dressing.
Tideswell Well Dressing.
Youlgreave Well Dressing.

JULY
Alport Love Feast (dates back to 1662), Heyridge Farm (off
    the A57), Snake Pass.
Ashbourne Highland Gathering.
Barnsley Vintage Vehicle Rally.
Baslow Carnival.
Bradwell Well Dressing.
Buxton International Arts Festival.
Buxton Jazz Festival.
Buxton Well Dressing.
Chesterfield Medieval Market.
Dore Well Dressing.
Dronfield Woodhouse Well Dressing.
Hathersage Gala.
Nostell Priory Country Fair.
Padley Pilgrimage, Grindleford.

AUGUST
Alton Towers, Last Night at the Proms.
Bakewell Agricultural Show.
Barlow Well Dressing.
Blyth Bank Holiday Market.
Chesterfield Bank Holiday Market.
Crich Transport Gathering, Crich Transport Museum.
Cromford Steam Rally.
Eyam Well Dressing.
Hope Sheepdog Trials and Agricultural Show.
Sherwood Forest Country Park Robin Hood Festival.
Wormhill Well dressing.
Worsborough Country Fair, Worsborough Country Park.

SEPTEMBER
Firework Display, Bolsover Castle.
Chatsworth Country Fair.

Chesterfield Well Dressing.
St Leger Festival, Doncaster Racecourse.
Glossop Victorian Weekend.
Longnor Well Dressing.
Longshaw Sheepdog Trials, near Hathersage.
Matlock Bath Illuminations.
Penistone Show.
R.A.F. Finningley Air Show.
Rotherham Show.
Wirksworth Clypping of the Church.

OCTOBER
Alton Towers, Halloween Thriller.

NOVEMBER
Abbeydale Industrial Hamlet, Working Days. Sheffield.
Alton Towers, Firework Spectacular.
Castleton, Christmas Lights.
RAC Ralley, Clumber Park.

DECEMBER
Peak Cavern, Castleton, Christmas Carols.
Great Hucklow, Christmas Lights.
Grenoside and Handsworth Longsword Dancing, Sheffield.
Matlock Bath, Raft Race.

USEFUL TELEPHONE NUMBERS

Tourist Information Centres:
Ashbourne   (0335) 43666
Bakewell   (0629) 813227
Barnsley   (0226) 206757
Buxton   (0298) 25106
Chesterfield   (0246) 207777
Doncaster   (0302) 734309
Glossop   (0457) 855920
Leek   (0538) 381000
Lincoln   (0522) 529828
Matlock   (0629) 55082
Ollerton   (0623) 824545
Retford   (0777) 860780
Rotherham   (0709) 823611
Sheffield   (0742) 734671/795901
Sherwood Forest   (0623) 824490
Wakefield   (0924) 295000
Worksop   (0909) 501148

Regional Tourist Boards, etc:
East Midlands Tourist Board   (0522) 531521
Heart of England Tourist Board   (0905) 763436
Yorkshire and Humberside Tourist Board   (0904) 707961
English Heritage   (091) 2611585
National Trust, East Midlands   (0909) 486411
National Trust, Yorkshire   (0904) 702021
Peak District National Park   (0629) 814321
Yorkshire and Humberside Museums Council   (0532) 638909